THE ULTIMATE BASKETBALL TRIVIA CHALLENGE

OVER 600 QUIZ QUESTIONS FOR
DIE-HARD BASKETBALL FANS

HANK PATTON

ISBN: 979-8-89095-058-1

Copyright © 2025 by Curious Press

ALL RIGHTS RESERVED

No part of this book may be reproduced, stored in a retrieval system, or transmitted in any form or by any means, electronic, mechanical, photocopying, recording, scanning, or otherwise, without the prior written permission of the publisher.

CONTENTS

INTRODUCTION 1

CHAPTER 1: BASKETBALL'S BEGINNINGS 3

CHAPTER 2: THE NATIONAL BASKETBALL LEAGUE 9

CHAPTER 3: BARNSTORMING 14

CHAPTER 4: OTHER EARLY LEAGUES 19

CHAPTER 5: COLLEGE AND INTERNATIONAL BEGINNINGS 24

CHAPTER 6: THE NBA IS BORN 29

CHAPTER 7: THE 1950S 34

CHAPTER 8: THE 1960S 39

CHAPTER 9: THE 1970S 44

CHAPTER 10: THE 1980S 49

CHAPTER 11: THE 1990S 54

CHAPTER 12: THE 2000S 59

CHAPTER 13: THE 2010S 64

CHAPTER 14: DREAM TEAMS 69

CHAPTER 15: TEAMS ON THE MOVE 74

CHAPTER 16: DIVISIONAL CHANGES 79

CHAPTER 17: THE EASTERN CONFERENCE 84

CHAPTER 18: THE WESTERN CONFERENCE 89

CHAPTER 19: ATLANTIC DIVISION 94

CHAPTER 20: CENTRAL DIVISION 99

CHAPTER 21: SOUTHEAST DIVISION.. 103

CHAPTER 22: NORTHWEST DIVISION 107

CHAPTER 23: PACIFIC DIVISION.. 112

CHAPTER 24: SOUTHWEST DIVISION.. 116

CHAPTER 25: THE NBA FINALS 120

CHAPTER 26: BASKETBALL HALL OF FAME.. 125

CHAPTER 27: SCORING CHAMPIONS 130

CHAPTER 28: THE SIXTH MAN AWARD.. 135

CHAPTER 29: BIGGEST NCAA TOURNAMENT MOMENTS 139

CHAPTER 30: UNBEATABLE RECORDS 144

CHAPTER 31: THE BIGGEST MOMENTS... 149

CHAPTER 32: THE ALL-STAR GAME 154

CHAPTER 33: SCANDALS AND MODERN HEADLINES 159

CHAPTER 34: BASKETBALL STATISTICS AND ACRONYMS 164

CONCLUSION 166

ATTENTION:

DO YOU WANT MY FUTURE BOOKS AT HEAVY DISCOUNTS AND EVEN FOR FREE?

HEAD OVER TO WWW.SECRETREADS.COM AND JOIN MY SECRET BOOK CLUB!

INTRODUCTION

The sport of basketball has come a long way from its humble beginnings in the 1890s. Over those years, the sport has grown and evolved from a school gymnasium to one of the most entertaining, popular competitions on the planet.

As players learned and developed skills to match the rules of the game, standout individuals began to challenge the norms. Rules changed, the game's popularity grew, and the country continued to watch as new generations of athletes broke records and entertained fans across the continent.

Today's game is faster than ever, and it features competitors that are not only the most athletic the game has ever seen, but also the most entertaining. In short, basketball has never been more popular.

With so many new eyes on the game, it can be difficult to recall the days when the sport was not as popular. It can also be a great conversation starter to challenge a fellow fan to a test of basketball knowledge. This book seeks to serve both of those purposes.

The early chapters of this trivia book will test the historians of the sport. It will cover the game's origins and how it has grown since then. Failed leagues will also be examined, as their impact on today's game is undeniable.

Most importantly, this book will challenge readers on their knowledge of each NBA team, their best players, and the most storied moments in the history of the game.

So, before beginning your journey through this book, ask yourself: Do you know more about basketball than anyone else? Will you know the answers to these basketball questions?

Grab your basketball friends and family or even crack this open on your own and prepare to put that basketball knowledge to the test! Are you going to hit a hot streak of three-pointers, or perhaps a lot of drives to the basket? Maybe you will need an assist from your teammates for some of these questions, too.

Either way, get ready for the tip-off!

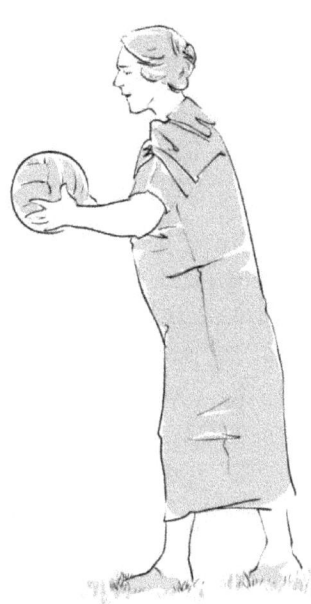

CHAPTER 1:
BASKETBALL'S BEGINNINGS

1. The game of basketball was invented by whom in December 1891?
    A. Eugene S. Libby
    B. James Naismith
    C. William Chase
    D. Frank Mahan

2. The game's inventor needed something for his students to do during what?
    A. Hot summers
    B. Rainy days
    C. Cold winters
    D. When a substitute was in charge

3. What kind of basket was used to catch the ball in the original iteration of the game?
    A. Peach
    B. Orange
    C. Apple
    D. Grape

4. How many rules were listed when the game was initially created?
    A. 10
    B. 11
    C. 12
    D. 13

5. In the original rules, how many consecutive fouls by one team awarded a point to their opponents?
    A. Three
    B. Four
    C. Five
    D. Six

6. Which of these features of modern basketball has an original rule tied to it?

A. Dribbling
   B. Passing
   C. Goaltending
   D. Jump ball

7. The fruit baskets were replaced with metal rims in what year?
   A. 1894
   B. 1899
   C. 1903
   D. 1906

8. In 1893, members of the YMCA took the game overseas, but not to which country?
   A. Japan
   B. England
   C. Persia
   D. India

9. The very first basketball game ever played was between two teams of how many players each?
   A. Five
   B. Six
   C. Seven
   D. Nine

10. The original rules did not allow what, making passing very important?
    A. Dribbling
    B. Overhand shooting
    C. Batting the ball
    D. Layups

11. The creator of this game was not native to the country where he invented it. Where was he from?
    A. Mexico
    B. Canada
    C. Germany
    D. Norway

12. The game was invented at the YMCA International Training School, but now it is called what?

A. Springfield College
   B. Emerson College
   C. Wheaton College
   D. Clark University

13. The original baskets were nailed to what, as there were no poles to hold them up?
    A. Balcony railings
    B. Gymnastics mats
    C. Soccer goal crossbars
    D. Flagpoles

14. The first basketball game finished with what final score?
    A. 0-0
    B. 1-0
    C. 2-0
    D. 2-1

15. The American Expeditionary Force helped spread the game all over Europe during which conflict?
    A. Italo-Turkish War
    B. Russo-Japanese War
    C. World War I
    D. Moro Wars

16. The creator of the game spent two years in which country during the war, helping to spread the game he invented?
    A. France
    B. Spain
    C. England
    D. Sweden

17. How many years after the game's invention in 1891 did the first professional league form?
    A. Five
    B. Six
    C. Seven
    D. Eight

18. The creator of the game went to which company for help creating the first basketball that wasn't just a soccer ball?

A. Rawlings
B. Spalding
C. Reebok
D. Adidas

CHAPTER 1 ANSWERS:
1. B. James Naismith. Dr. Naismith was a 31-year-old grad student at the time.
2. C. Cold winters. Naismith needed an indoor game that didn't require much to set up.
3. A. Peach. The basket also didn't have the bottom cut out, at first.
4. D. 13. The original game had 15-minute halves.
5. A. Three. Rules like these make it amazingly easy to believe that this game started in a school gym.
6. C. Goaltending. Even back then, defenders could not touch their own basket!
7. D. 1906. The soccer ball initially used was replaced much earlier, in 1894.
8. B. England. Each of the other countries listed experienced basketball that year from the YMCA ambassadors.
9. D. Nine. It is likely that all nine players were on the court for each team at the same time.
10. A. Dribbling. Players had to immediately stop running upon possessing the ball.
11. B. Canada. James Naismith was working in the United States at the time.
12. A. Springfield College. A little over 2,000 students attend every year.
13. A. Balcony railings. The janitor had to retrieve the ball when a team scored.
14. B. 1-0. Scoring was quite difficult for the new players.
15. C. World War I. Americans were able to teach the rules to many European participants.
16. A. France. The YMCA was popular around the world, helping the game spread faster.
17. C. Seven. The first pro league formed in 1898.
18. B. Spalding. All of the choices in this question existed back then, though.

Did You Know?
Naismith would go on to create the University of Kansas basketball program.

CHAPTER 2:
THE NATIONAL BASKETBALL LEAGUE

1. The first iteration of the National Basketball League formed in 1898 and lasted how many full seasons?

   A. Three
   B. Four
   C. Five
   D. Six

2. The league's first game was played in front of how many fans at Textile Hall in Philadelphia?

   A. 500
   B. 900
   C. 1,100
   D. 1,400

3. The National Basketball League's first season featured how many teams?

   A. Six
   B. Seven
   C. Eight
   D. Ten

4. Of the teams that started the season, how many of the teams folded before the season's end?

   A. One
   B. Two
   C. Three
   D. Four

5. Which of these teams won the first season of the National Basketball League?

   A. Millville Glass Blowers
   B. Camden Electrics
   C. Clover Wheelmen
   D. Trenton Nationals

6. The league's second season also featured six teams, but which one had to drop out this time?
   A. New York Wanderers
   B. Bristol Pile Drivers
   C. Chester, PA
   D. Pennsylvania Bicycle Club

7. The third NBL season featured seven teams, but which one emerged victorious?
   A. Camden Skeeters
   B. New York Wanderers
   C. Bristol Pile Drivers
   D. Burlington, NJ

8. The 1901–1902 season, which is considered the most successful season in terms of the league's stability, featured how many games per team?
   A. 30
   B. 35
   C. 40
   D. 45

9. During the 1902–1903 season, the owner of the Burlington Shoe Pegs fired his players and then bought which team to represent Burlington?
   A. New York Wanderers
   B. Bristol Pile Drivers
   C. Trenton Potters
   D. Camden Electrics

10. True or False: Phillies manager Frank Morgenweck would eventually be inducted into the Basketball Hall of Fame.

11. The Camden Electrics won the 1903 championship with what winning percentage?
    A. .750
    B. .800
    C. .850
    D. .900

12. How many teams committed to the final season of the NBL?
    A. Two

B. Three
   C. Four
   D. Five

13. The Camden Electrics were in first place when the league was disbanded on what date?

    A. January 4, 1904
    B. February 13, 1904
    C. February 19, 1904
    D. March 1, 1904

14. True or False: Over the six seasons in the league, the Camden Electrics won three titles.

15. True or False: The Camden Electrics and the Trenton Nationals won the same number of titles.

16. True or False: The Millville Glass Blowers and St. Bridget's Biddies both played in the final season of the league.

17. Another version of the National Basketball League would emerge how many years after this league folded in 1904?

    A. 25
    B. 31
    C. 33
    D. 37

18. In the 1900–1901 season, how many of the seven teams finished with a record of .500 or better?

    A. Three
    B. Four
    C. Five
    D. Six

CHAPTER 2 ANSWERS:

1. C. Five. The league disbanded halfway through the sixth season.
2. B. 900. It was a small but promising start.
3. A. Six. It was a small group, and not every team would finish the season.
4. B. Two. Those two teams didn't even last a month.
5. D. Trenton Nationals. They finished with an 18-2-1 record.
6. C. Chester, PA. Millville joined to fill the vacancy after electing not to participate at the beginning of the season.
7. B. New York Wanderers. They won the league by three games.
8. C. 40. Bristol won the title with a 28-12 record.
9. B. Bristol Pile Drivers. The Philadelphia Phillies did the same thing to the Wilmington Peaches.
10. True. His brother coached the Camden Electrics, who won the 1903 championship.
11. B. .800. They had a 36-9 record.
12. D. Five. It was an omen that the league would not survive.
13. A. January 4, 1904. Investors sued Camden's coach after the league folded.
14. False. Camden won the last two titles.
15. True. Both teams won twice.
16. True. Team names were fascinating back then.
17. C. 33. The next iteration would also last much longer.
18. C. Five. One of the two teams under .500 didn't finish the season.

Did You Know?

The National Basketball League only featured teams from the northeast region of the United States.

CHAPTER 3: BARNSTORMING

1. A popular barnstorming team of the 1910s and 1920s shared their name with which current NBA team?

    A. Lakers
    B. Celtics
    C. Knicks
    D. Pistons

2. True or False: The New York Original Celtics organization is the same one that now runs the Boston Celtics.

3. True or False: While traveling around the country, the Original Celtics would travel up to 150,000 miles per year.

4. How many different leagues did the Original Celtics compete in during their 20 years of competition?

    A. One
    B. Two
    C. Three
    D. Four

5. The Original Celtics challenged which team in 1923, hoping to use a victory to declare themselves national champions, but were refused?

    A. Franklin Wonder Five
    B. Harlem Globetrotters
    C. Brooklyn Arcadians
    D. Columbia Lions

6. True or False: Dutch Dehnert of the Original Celtics is credited by some with introducing the modern concept of jump shooting.

7. True or False: Original Celtics player Nat Holman was known for his ballhandling skills.

8. John Beckman of the Original Celtics was known as the "_____ of Basketball."

    A. Cy Young
    B. Willie Mays

C. Babe Ruth
D. Hank Aaron

9. After playing one season in the Eastern Basketball League, the Original Celtics played in which league?

   A. American Basketball League
   B. Metropolitan Basketball League
   C. National Basketball League
   D. National Basketball Association

10. True or False: The Original Celtics dropped out of the Metropolitan Basketball League after winning their first six games.

11. True or False: The Original Celtics won two championships in the American Basketball League.

12. The Globetrotters of today, founded in 1926, started in which city?

    A. New York City
    B. Harlem
    C. Philadelphia
    D. Chicago

13. Over their 98 years of history, how many championships have the Globetrotters collected?

    A. 50
    B. 75
    C. 100
    D. 150

14. True or False: The first Black player drafted to the NBA was a member of the Globetrotters.

15. True or False: The Globetrotters never won the World Professional Basketball Tournament.

16. The Globetrotters famously beat which team in 1948, two years before Black players were allowed into the NBA?

    A. Minneapolis Lakers
    B. Rochester Royals
    C. Philadelphia Warriors
    D. St. Louis Bombers

17. Despite pro basketball never attracting more than 9,000 fans, the famous Globetrotters game in 1948 had a crowd of how many spectators?

   A. 12,000
   B. 15,000
   C. 17,000
   D. 18,000

18. True or False: The more entertaining side of the Globetrotters is credited to Reece "Goose" Tatum, who joined the team in 1941.

CHAPTER 3 ANSWERS:

1. B. Celtics. The New York Original Celtics were a powerhouse team around the country.
2. False. The two are not related, though today's Celtics may have used the name as inspiration.
3. True. The team would play 150–200 games per year.
4. C. Three. The team only played in leagues for six years of their existence.
5. A. Franklin Wonder Five. The team declined, citing fatigue.
6. False. He is credited with introducing pivot play.
7. True. He would later coach CCNY to multiple national championships.
8. C. Babe Ruth. Beckman and his teammates dominated the leagues in which they played.
9. B. Metropolitan Basketball League. The team would only play one season there as well.
10. False. The team won 12 straight games without a loss, then they left the league.
11. True. Out of the five seasons they played they won two championships.
12. D. Chicago. The team was only based there for two years.
13. B. 75. However, the team rarely played worthy opponents.
14. True. Chuck Cooper was not the first Black player to sign an NBA contract, though.
15. False. The team won it in 1940.
16. A. Minneapolis Lakers. They won on a buzzer-beater.
17. D. 18,000. It was a legendary moment in basketball.
18. True. It changed the direction and viability of the team for years to come.

Did You Know?

The Harlem Globetrotters confused crowds in Moscow when they played nine games there in 1959.

CHAPTER 4:
OTHER EARLY LEAGUES

1. The American Basketball League was one of the first pro league attempts in the US, beginning in which year?

    A. 1924
    B. 1925
    C. 1926
    D. 1927

2. Joseph Carr, who founded the ABL, was also the president of which league?

    A. National Hockey League
    B. National Football League
    C. National Basketball League
    D. Professional Golfers' Association

3. The first ABL champions came from which city?

    A. Brooklyn
    B. Fort Wayne
    C. Cleveland
    D. Rochester

4. In the 13 seasons of the Eastern Basketball League, which is the only team to successfully defend their championship?

    A. Camden Skeeters
    B. Germantown Geraniums
    C. Greystock Greys
    D. Jasper Jewels

5. True or False: The last team to win an EBL championship was the New York Original Celtics.

6. True or False: The Metropolitan Basketball League finished seven seasons, and four were won by teams from Brooklyn.

7. How long did the MBL last after the Visitations joined the ABL?

    A. One week

B. Two weeks
   C. Three weeks
   D. Four weeks

8. The New York State Basketball League awarded their final championship in 1924 to which team?
   A. Glens Falls Maroons
   B. Kingston Colonials
   C. Cohoes Cohosiers
   D. Albany Senators

9. True or False: The Schenectady Dorpians won three straight NYSBL league titles.

10. True or False: The Central Basketball League ran for six seasons, from 1906 to 1912.

11. The final championship won in the American Basketball League went to which team?
    A. Wilkes-Barre Barons
    B. Scranton Miners
    C. Trenton Tigers
    D. Manchester British-Americans

12. The Pennsylvania State Basketball League lasted for how many seasons?
    A. Five
    B. Six
    C. Seven
    D. Eight

13. True or False: Pittson was the only team to win two championships in the Pennsylvania State Basketball League.

14. True or False: The Wilmington Blue Bombers were the only team to win both halves of the ABL season, a feat they accomplished in 1942.

15. The leading scorer in any single season of ABL play was which player of the Paterson Crescents?
    A. Dick Holub
    B. Joe Colone
    C. Elmore Morgenthaler

D. Johnny Ezersky

16. How many ABL scoring leaders have been inducted into the Basketball Hall of Fame?

    A. One
    B. Two
    C. Three
    D. Four

17. True or False: The Philadelphia Sphas won seven championships in ten seasons competing in the ABL.

18. True or False: Ray Felix had the highest points per game average of any ABL player, with 22.0 in 1952–53.

CHAPTER 4 ANSWERS:

1. B. 1925. The league could not convince the New York Original Celtics to join, at least not initially.
2. B. National Football League. Many NFL owners would also own teams in this league.
3. C. Cleveland. They won three of the first five titles.
4. C. Greystock Greys. The team won in 1916 and 1917.
5. True. They won in 1922, and the league didn't finish the 1923 season.
6. True. The Brooklyn Visitations won three, and the Brooklyn Dodgers won one.
7. B. Two weeks. It was a poor ending, but basketball leagues at the time were fickle.
8. A. Glens Falls Maroons. The league's early years were dominated by the Troy Trojans.
9. False. The team won two in a row, in 1916 and 1917.
10. True. It did well until competition from the Eastern and New York Leagues drove them out.
11. D. Manchester British-Americans. They defeated Wilkes-Barre 1-0 to capture the final crown.
12. C. Seven. Their final season was in 1921.
13. True. Their success did not help them branch out to other leagues, though.
14. True. Every other season required a championship between the winners of the two season halves.
15. A. Dick Holub. He scored 835 points in 41 games during the 1948–49 season.
16. B. Two. Bennie Borgmann and Bobby McDermott.
17. True. Their first was in 1935–36, their seventh in 1944–45.
18. True. He scored 618 points in 28 games.

Did You Know?

The Great Depression caused the league to suspend operations for two seasons.

CHAPTER 5:
COLLEGE AND INTERNATIONAL BEGINNINGS

1. One of the first recorded games between two college teams resulted in a Minnesota A&M victory over Hamline University by what score?

    A. 3-0
    B. 9-3
    C. 10-0
    D. 11-6

2. The first college game using modern rules took place between the University of Iowa and which school?

    A. University of Chicago
    B. University of Nebraska
    C. University of Missouri
    D. University of New York

3. True or False: The first tournament that featured only college teams was during the 1904 Olympics, won by Hiram College.

4. True or False: The 1922 National Intercollegiate Basketball Tournament was the first stand-alone, post-season tournament, won by Wabash College.

5. Which organization was the first to have a regularly occurring national college championship?

    A. National Invitation Tournament
    B. National Association of Intercollegiate Athletics
    C. National Collegiate Athletic Association
    D. Amateur Athletic Union

6. Which of the six participants won the first NIT tournament in 1938?

    A. Colorado
    B. Long Island
    C. Temple
    D. Oklahoma A&M

7. True or False: The first NCAA tournament, in 1939, was won by the Oregon Webfoots.

8. True or False: In 1940, the NCAA created a rule that teams could not compete in both the NCAA and NIT tournaments.

9. The International Basketball Federation was founded in which country?

    A. Latvia
    B. Greece
    C. Argentina
    D. Switzerland

10. The first men's World Cup in basketball took place in which year?

    A. 1944
    B. 1950
    C. 1956
    D. 1960

11. True or False: As of 2024, the United States and Germany are tied for the most gold medals in FIBA World Cup tournaments.

12. True or False: The first team to win two FIBA World Cup tournaments in a row was Brazil, in 1959 and 1963.

13. The highest points average by a player in any tournament was accomplished by a player from which country in 1990?

    A. Greece
    B. Brazil
    C. South Korea
    D. Argentina

14. Nikos Galis holds the record for the highest scoring average over multiple tournaments, with how many points?

    A. 31.0
    B. 31.8
    C. 32.6
    D. 33.3

15. True or False: The longest FIBA game required three overtime periods, back in 2006.

16. True or False: The oldest player to participate in the FIBA World Cup tournament was Eduardo Mingas, of Angola.

17. The biggest margin of victory in a FIBA World Cup match is how many points?

    A. 70
    B. 79
    C. 90
    D. 92

18. The player with the most points in a single FIBA World Cup game is Hur Jae of South Korea, with how many points?

    A. 54
    B. 53
    C. 52
    D. 48

CHAPTER 5 ANSWERS:

1. B. 9-3. The game took place in February of 1895, and there were nine players per side.
2. A. University of Chicago. Chicago won 15-12.
3. True. It was played as a demonstration sport, to promote its play around the world.
4. True. The tourney featured champions from six major college conferences.
5. B. National Association of Intercollegiate Athletics. It was quickly overtaken by the NIT.
6. C. Temple. They defeated Colorado to win.
7. True. They defeated the Ohio State Buckeyes.
8. False. The rule was created in 1950, paving the way for the NCAA to take the lead over the NIT.
9. D. Switzerland. There were eight national federations in attendance for its creation in 1932.
10. B. 1950. Argentina defeated the U.S.A. to win the first tournament.
11. False. The United States is tied with Yugoslavia, both with five.
12. True. Brazil has not won since then.
13. B. Brazil. Oscar Schmidt averaged 34.6 points in the 1990 tournament.
14. C. 32.6. The Greek player kept that average over ten games.
15. True. Germany defeated Angola in the Preliminary Round.
16. True. He was 40 years and 214 days old during the 2019 tournament.
17. D. 92. The Soviet Union defeated the Central African Republic in the 1974 tournament.
18. A. 54. He scored those points against Egypt in the 1990 tournament.

Did You Know?

Only conference champions were allowed to compete in the NCAA Tournament until 1975.

CHAPTER 6:
THE NBA IS BORN

1. The Basketball Association of America was founded how many years before it became the National Basketball Association?

    A. One
    B. Two
    C. Three
    D. Four

2. In what many consider the first NBA game ever played, the Toronto Huskies hosted which team?

    A. Detroit Falcons
    B. New York Knickerbockers
    C. Cleveland Rebels
    D. Chicago Stags

3. True or False: Ernie Calverley of the Providence Steamrollers led the BAA during the 1946–47 season with 202 assists.

4. True or False: Before the 1948 season, four NBL teams transferred to the BAA, making it the premier destination for players entering the league from college.

5. In August of 1949, the remaining NBL teams merged into the BAA. How many teams made that move?

    A. Four
    B. Five
    C. Six
    D. Seven

6. The Baltimore Bullets defeated which team in the finals to capture the 1948 BAA championship?

    A. Philadelphia Warriors
    B. New York Knicks
    C. Boston Celtics
    D. St. Louis Bombers

7. True or False: Max Zaslofsky led the BAA in scoring during the 1947-48 season with 1,007 points.

8. True or False: The Washington Capitols won the final championship of the BAA, before it became the NBA.

9. Which team finished with the worst record during the 1948-49 season?

    A. Indianapolis Jets
    B. Fort Wayne Pistons
    C. Boston Celtics
    D. Providence Steamrollers

10. George Mikan was playing for which team when he led the league in scoring during the 1948-49 season?

    A. Rochester Royals
    B. Washington Capitols
    C. Minneapolis Lakers
    D. Fort Wayne Pistons

11. True or False: Arnie Risen of the Rochester Royals led the 1948-49 season with a .423 shooting percentage.

12. True or False: The Providence Steamrollers and Indianapolis Jets finished at the bottom of the 1948-49 season, then both folded.

13. The 1949-50 season, the first with the NBA name, had how many teams competing?

    A. 15
    B. 16
    C. 17
    D. 18

14. Three NBA teams finished the 1949-50 season with 51 wins. Which of these teams did not?

    A. Syracuse Nationals
    B. New York Knicks
    C. Minneapolis Lakers
    D. Rochester Royals

15. True or False: Syracuse lost to Minneapolis in the finals despite having a bye in the semifinals.

16. True or False: Dick McGuire led the league in assists during the 1949-50 season with 386.

17. Which of these teams was the expansion team in 1949–50?
    A. Indianapolis Olympians
    B. Anderson Packers
    C. Sheboygan Red Skins
    D. Waterloo Hawks

18. True or False: At the end of the 1949–50 season, five teams left the league.

CHAPTER 6 ANSWERS:

1. C. Three. It merged with the National Basketball League.
2. B. New York Knickerbockers. It was a BAA game, but it is still considered part of NBA history.
3. True. However, the Steamrollers did not make the playoffs that year.
4. True. It established the BAA as the dominant league after a couple of years of competition with the NBL.
5. C. Six. Syracuse, Anderson, Tri-Cities, Sheboygan, Denver, and Waterloo all made the move at that time.
6. A. Philadelphia Warriors. Baltimore won the series 4-2.
7. True. Zaslofsky's Chicago Stags lost to Baltimore in the playoffs.
8. False. The Capitols lost to the Minneapolis Lakers.
9. D. Providence Steamrollers. They only won 12 games, with 48 losses.
10. C. Minneapolis Lakers. He scored 1,698 points that season.
11. True. Rochester lost in the semifinals to Minneapolis, though.
12. True. They were transfers from the NBL but didn't last long.
13. C. 17. The six NBL transfers joined the ten surviving teams and one expansion team.
14. B. New York Knicks. They had 40 wins that season, comfortably in a playoff position.
15. True. Syracuse waited for Anderson and Minneapolis to battle for a spot in the finals.
16. True. He played for the Knicks, who lost to Syracuse in the division finals.
17. A. Indianapolis Olympians. They would have the best record in their division that season, too.
18. False. Six teams left, shrinking the league from 17 to 11.

Did You Know?

The NBA did not start tracking rebounds until 1950.

CHAPTER 7: THE 1950S

1. True or False: The longest game in NBA history took place in January of 1951, and it took four overtimes to find a winner.

2. The lowest-scoring game in league history took place in November of 1950 between the Lakers and which team?

   A. Fort Wayne Pistons
   B. Rochester Royals
   C. Syracuse Nationals
   D. New York Knicks

3. The first NBA All-Star Game resulted in which player earning MVP honors?

   A. Andy Phillip
   B. Ed Macauley
   C. George Mikan
   D. Jim Pollard

4. True or False: The Washington Capitols folded halfway through the 1950–51 season.

5. True or False: Earl Lloyd was the first Black player to play in the NBA.

6. Two players tied for the most rebounds in the 1951–52 season, but how many did they each get?

   A. 660
   B. 770
   C. 880
   D. 990

7. Which Royals player impressed from the free throw line, shooting .904 in the 1951–52 season?

   A. Bobby Wanzer
   B. Paul Arizin
   C. Jim Pollard
   D. Bob Davies

8. True or False: The Lakers won another championship in 1953, defeating the Knicks in five games.

9. True or False: Don Meineke won the first Rookie of the Year award in 1953.

10. Which team folded before the beginning of the 1953–54 season, shrinking the league to nine teams?
    A. Syracuse Nationals
    B. Rochester Royals
    C. Baltimore Bullets
    D. Indianapolis Olympians

11. Which of these teams did not advance through the Division Round Robin Semifinals, which had not been used in the league before the 1954 playoffs?
    A. Minneapolis Lakers
    B. Boston Celtics
    C. Fort Wayne Pistons
    D. Syracuse Nationals

12. True or False: The NBA introduced a 30-second shot clock to start the 1954–55 season.

13. True or False: The Baltimore Bullets folded after 14 games of the 1954–55 season.

14. In the 1955–56 season, the Philadelphia Warriors defeated which team to win the championship?
    A. Rochester Royals
    B. Fort Wayne Pistons
    C. St. Louis Hawks
    D. Syracuse Nationals

15. 1956 marked the first time the NBA selected a league MVP. Who did they pick?
    A. Bob Pettit
    B. Bob Cousy
    C. Neil Johnston
    D. Bill Sharman

16. True or False: The Boston Celtics won the 1957 NBA Finals over the St. Louis Hawks in four games.

17. True or False: Despite going seven games to crown a champion, neither team lost a playoff game on their way to the Finals.

18. The 1959 NBA Finals marked the first of how many consecutive titles for the Boston Celtics?

    A. Six
    B. Seven
    C. Eight
    D. Nine

CHAPTER 7 ANSWERS:

1. False. It took six overtimes.
2. A. Fort Wayne Pistons. The Pistons beat the Lakers 19-18.
3. B. Ed Macauley. The East defeated the West 111-94.
4. True. It left the league with ten teams.
5. True. He played for the Washington Capitols before they folded.
6. C. 880. Larry Foust and Mel Hutchins tied for the honor.
7. A. Bobby Wanzer. His season with the Royals also helped him earn All-NBA Second Team honors.
8. True. The Lakers also had the best record in the regular season.
9. True. He played for the Pistons that season.
10. D. Indianapolis Olympians. The Western Division had four teams; the East had five.
11. C. Fort Wayne Pistons. They lost four games against Rochester and Minneapolis.
12. False. The shot clock was only 24 seconds.
13. True. It marks the last time an NBA team folded, as of 2024.
14. B. Fort Wayne Pistons. The Warriors won the series in five games.
15. A. Bob Pettit. He led the league in both points and rebounds that season.
16. False. The Celtics needed seven games to defeat the Hawks.
17. True. In fact, every other series in the playoffs that year was a sweep.
18. C. Eight. It was one of the most dominant stretches in the history of American sports.

Did You Know?

The Detroit Pistons hosted the All-Star Game in 1959, just one season after moving to the area from Fort Wayne.

CHAPTER 8:
THE 1960S

1. True or False: Wilt Chamberlain won the 1960 All-Star Game MVP award as a rookie.

2. True or False: The Celtics won 59 of their 75 regular season games in 1959–60 on their way to another NBA title.

3. Though Chamberlain led in points and assists during the 1960–61 season, which rival of his won the league MVP?

   A. Oscar Robertson
   B. Bob Pettit
   C. Bill Russell
   D. Bob Cousy

4. Of the eight teams competing during the 1960–61 season, how many teams finished with a winning record?

   A. Two
   B. Three
   C. Four
   D. Five

5. True or False: Wilt Chamberlain scored an NBA-record 100 points in a win over the Detroit Pistons during the 1961–62 season.

6. True or False: Oscar Robertson became the first player in NBA history to average a triple-double throughout a season, during the 1961–62 year.

7. The Celtics beat which team to win their fifth straight title in 1963?

   A. San Francisco Warriors
   B. Los Angeles Lakers
   C. St. Louis Hawks
   D. Detroit Pistons

8. Which Lakers player was named to the 1963 All-NBA First Team in the guard position?

   A. Jerry West
   B. Elgin Baylor

C. Frank Selvy
   D. Dick Barnett

9. True or False: Alex Hannum won the first NBA Coach of the Year Award in 1964.

10. True or False: Boston beat the Cincinnati Royals 4-1 in the Eastern Division Finals before beating the Warriors by the same margin in the 1964 NBA Finals.

11. The Celtics won 62 games in 1964–65, but how many did they lose?
    A. 18
    B. 20
    C. 22
    D. 24

12. During the 1965–66 season, Chamberlain and the 76ers finished how many games ahead of the eventual champion Celtics?
    A. One
    B. Two
    C. Three
    D. Four

13. True or False: Oscar Robertson led the league in assists during the 1965–66 season.

14. True or False: The NBA expanded to ten teams in 1966 as the Atlanta Hawks joined.

15. The 1967 All-Star Game was played at which arena?
    A. Horse Palace
    B. Palace of Auburn Hills
    C. Pig Palace
    D. Cow Palace

16. Though Chamberlain won the MVP in 1967, who led the league in scoring?
    A. Dave Bing
    B. Guy Rodgers
    C. Rick Barry
    D. Adrian Smith

17. True or False: Seattle and San Diego both joined the league in 1967, the same year that the American Basketball Association began play.

18. True or False: Dave Bing led the league in scoring during the 1967–68 season while playing for the Cincinnati Royals.

CHAPTER 8 ANSWERS:

1. True. Wilt's dominance was great, but Boston would prevent him from winning many titles.
2. True. They finished ten games ahead of Philadelphia in the East.
3. C. Bill Russell. It was a great rivalry that lasted for more than a decade.
4. B. Three. Boston, Philadelphia, and St. Louis were the strongest teams by far.
5. False. The game was against the New York Knicks, not the Pistons.
6. True. He still didn't win the MVP, though.
7. B. Los Angeles Lakers. The Celtics won in six games.
8. A. Jerry West. He only had two years of NBA experience at that point.
9. True. He coached the San Francisco Warriors.
10. True. The Royals only finished four games behind the Celtics during the season, so many expected the series to be closer.
11. A. 18. There were 80 games in the regular season during this time.
12. A. One. They won 55 games to Boston's 54, but still couldn't get by them in the playoffs.
13. True. He had 847 of them that year.
14. False. The Chicago Bulls joined the league that year.
15. D. Cow Palace. It was the home of the San Francisco Warriors.
16. C. Rick Barry. He scored 2,775 points for the Warriors.
17. True. It was a large expansion of basketball.
18. False. He played for the Detroit Pistons.

Did You Know?
Besides 1967, the Celtics won every championship during the 1960s.

CHAPTER 9:
THE 1970S

1. In only their second year, the Milwaukee Bucks won how many games during the 1969–70 season?

    A. 45
    B. 52
    C. 56
    D. 59

2. The 1970 NBA championship was won by which team, defeating the Lakers in seven games?

    A. Boston Celtics
    B. Milwaukee Bucks
    C. New York Knicks
    D. Baltimore Bullets

3. True or False: Three teams joined the NBA in 1970, making the league 17 teams.

4. True or False: For the first time in NBA history, two players were awarded the Rookie of the Year Award in 1971.

5. The Lakers won a record number of regular season games in 1971–72. How many did they win?

    A. 66
    B. 67
    C. 68
    D. 69

6. The 1972 playoffs marked the first time which team did not reach the postseason?

    A. Philadelphia 76ers
    B. New York Knicks
    C. Boston Celtics
    D. Detroit Pistons

7. True or False: The Cincinnati Royals moved in 1972 but split their home games between two cities: Kansas City and Omaha.

8. True or False: Dave Cowens of the Celtics was named MVP in 1973, though his team lost in the conference finals that season.

9. Which player won the All-Star Game MVP in 1974, though his team did not reach the NBA Finals later that year?

    A. John Havlicek
    B. Elmore Smith
    C. Bob McAdoo
    D. Bob Lanier

10. Bob McAdoo led the league in points per game and field goal percentage during the 1973–74 season, the first player to accomplish the feat since when?

    A. 1965
    B. 1966
    C. 1967
    D. 1968

11. True or False: The New Orleans Jazz joined the NBA at the beginning of the 1974–75 season.

12. True or False: The Lakers missed the playoffs in 1975 for the first time since moving to California.

13. After spending a few seasons split between two cities, the Kings made which city their home in 1975?

    A. Omaha
    B. Kansas City
    C. Los Angeles
    D. Sacramento

14. Which aptly named player led the 1975–76 season in both steals and assists per game?

    A. Kareem Abdul-Jabbar
    B. Wes Unseld
    C. Slick Watts
    D. Bob McAdoo

15. True or False: When the ABA merged with the NBA in 1976, it added six teams to the league.

16. True or False: The Portland Trail Blazers defeated the Philadelphia 76ers to win the NBA title in 1977.

17. Bill Walton won the league MVP but missed 22 games of the season because of what?

    A. Broken finger
    B. Broken arm
    C. Broken foot
    D. Broken toe

18. The Seattle SuperSonics won the 1979 NBA championship, which was the last time any team from the Northwest Division won the title for how many years?

    A. 33
    B. 44
    C. 55
    D. 66

CHAPTER 9 ANSWERS:

1. C. 56. Rookie Lew Alcindor, also known as Kareem Abdul-Jabbar, played a crucial role in those wins.
2. C. New York Knicks. The Knicks also had the best record that year.
3. True. Portland, Buffalo, and Cleveland all had teams.
4. True. Dave Cowens and Geoff Petrie both received the honor.
5. D. 69. The record stood until 1996.
6. A. Philadelphia 76ers. They missed the cut off by six games.
7. True. The team finished ten games under .500, last in their division.
8. True. However, the Celtics would return to glory soon enough.
9. D. Bob Lanier. His Pistons struggled to overcome Chicago in the first round.
10. B. 1966. Chamberlain did it during the 1965–66 season.
11. True. However, they finished at the bottom of the league.
12. True. They finished last in the Western Conference.
13. B. Kansas City. They missed the playoffs that year, not a great start to their new home.
14. C. Slick Watts. His great play helped Seattle earn the second seed in the Western Conference.
15. False. It added four teams: The Spurs, Pacers, Nuggets, and Nets.
16. True. Bill Walton earned Finals MVP for his efforts.
17. C. Broken foot. Many expected Portland to repeat as champions until his injury occurred.
18. B. 44. The Denver Nuggets broke the drought in 2023.

Did You Know?

The 1979 Finals would be the last not to feature either the Lakers or Celtics for more than ten years.

CHAPTER 10:
THE 1980S

1. True or False: The 1979–80 season was the first to use the three-point field goal.

2. True or False: Both Magic Johnson and Larry Bird played their rookie seasons during the 1979–80 campaign.

3. When the Dallas Mavericks joined the league in 1980, the Bucks and which team moved to the Eastern Conference?

   A. Chicago Bulls
   B. Houston Rockets
   C. San Antonio Spurs
   D. Cleveland Cavaliers

4. Julius Erving earned league MVP honors in 1981 while playing for which team?

   A. Boston Celtics
   B. Utah Jazz
   C. Philadelphia 76ers
   D. Houston Rockets

5. True or False: Magic Johnson won his second Finals MVP in 1982 before the age of 23.

6. True or False: The 1981–82 Denver Nuggets are the only team in NBA history to score 100 points in every regular season game while also allowing 100 points in every regular season game.

7. The Milwaukee Bucks swept which team in the 1983 playoffs; a team that had never been swept before?

   A. Los Angeles Lakers
   B. Boston Celtics
   C. Detroit Pistons
   D. Philadelphia 76ers

8. 1983 was the first year that the NBA gave awards for Defensive Player of the Year and which award?

   A. Sportsmanship Award

B. Community Impact Award
   C. Comeback Award
   D. Sixth Man Award

9. True or False: The Mavericks reached the playoffs for the first time in 1984, defeating the SuperSonics in the first round.

10. True or False: The 1984 playoffs were the first to include eight teams from each conference.

11. Michael Jordan became the only rookie to lead his team in how many statistics?
    A. One
    B. Two
    C. Three
    D. Four

12. Kareem became the oldest Finals MVP in 1985. How old was he?
    A. 35
    B. 36
    C. 37
    D. 38

13. True or False: The 1985–86 Celtics set the NBA record with a home record of 40 wins and one loss.

14. True or False: Detlef Schrempf was the first German player to play in the NBA, entering the league in 1985.

15. With Mychal Thompson added to the roster, the Lakers became the first team to have how many first overall draft picks on a squad?
    A. Two
    B. Three
    C. Four
    D. Five

16. This legendary player became the first to enter the 50-40-90 club in 1987.
    A. Larry Bird
    B. Michael Jordan
    C. Magic Johnson
    D. Julius Erving

17. True or False: Michael Jordan won the 1988 scoring title, Defensive Player of the Year, and league MVP, the only player to do so.

18. True or False: The 1987–88 Spurs were the last team to lose 50 games and still make the playoffs.

CHAPTER 10 ANSWERS:

1. True. The game would never be played the same again.
2. True. Larry would win Rookie of the Year, but Magic would win Finals MVP.
3. A. Chicago Bulls. The Bulls would finish second in the division that year.
4. C. Philadelphia 76ers. He couldn't help Philadelphia get by Boston that season, though.
5. True. His dominance started early.
6. True. It did not translate to playoff success, though.
7. B. Boston Celtics. Milwaukee would lose to the eventual champions, the Philadelphia 76ers.
8. D. Sixth Man Award. The first winner was Bobby Jones of Philadelphia.
9. True. They lost to the Lakers in the second round.
10. True. It was also the first to increase first-round matchups from three games to five.
11. D. Four. He led the Bulls in points, assists, rebounds, and steals.
12. D. 38. The Lakers defeated the Celtics in the Finals.
13. True. The record was tied in 2016 by the Spurs.
14. True. He'd also be the first European All-Star, but not until 1993.
15. C. Four. It was a dominant roster up and down.
16. A. Larry Bird. It represented his balanced game.
17. True. His domination was apparent around the league.
18. True. Today's game is much more competitive.

Did You Know?

The 1989 playoffs ended with a Pistons sweep over the Los Angeles Lakers.

CHAPTER 11:
THE 1990S

1. The 1990-91 season was the first in ten years that the Lakers didn't win their division. Who did?

    A. Phoenix Suns
    B. Portland Trail Blazers
    C. Golden State Warriors
    D. Los Angeles Clippers

2. The NBA became the first league to play a game outside of North America. Where did the Jazz and Suns play to open the season in 1990?

    A. China
    B. Germany
    C. Japan
    D. Spain

3. True or False: The Chicago Bulls won the 1992 NBA Finals over the Utah Jazz.

4. True or False: The 1991-92 Milwaukee Bucks missed the playoffs for the first time since 1979.

5. Of the four expansion teams that joined in the late 1980s, which one was the first to win a playoff series in 1993?

    A. Orlando Magic
    B. Minnesota Timberwolves
    C. Charlotte Hornets
    D. Miami Heat

6. The Bulls won their third straight championship in 1993, defeating which team?

    A. Utah Jazz
    B. Phoenix Suns
    C. Los Angeles Lakers
    D. San Antonio Spurs

7. True or False: In 1993, the Orlando Magic became the first team to win the first overall pick two years in a row.

8. True or False: The last quadruple-double to take place in an NBA game happened in February of 1994.

9. Which team became the lowest seed to ever win the NBA Finals, doing so in 1995?

   A. Orlando Magic
   B. Houston Rockets
   C. Indiana Pacers
   D. San Antonio Spurs

10. Though the Hornets were the first late 1980s expansion team to win a playoff series, which one was the first to reach the NBA Finals?

    A. Minnesota Timberwolves
    B. Miami Heat
    C. Orlando Magic
    D. San Antonio Spurs

11. True or False: In 1995, the NBA added two Canadian teams for the first time since 1947.

12. True or False: In 1996, Michael Jordan became the only player to win the Finals MVP four times.

13. Allen Iverson set a rookie record during the 1996–97 season by scoring 40 or more points in how many games?

    A. Three
    B. Four
    C. Five
    D. Six

14. Which general manager took over coaching duties for the 1996–97 Spurs after they started a dismal 3-15?

    A. Bob Hill
    B. Gregg Popovich
    C. Larry Brown
    D. Phil Jackson

15. True or False: Kobe Bryant became the youngest All-Star starter at 19 years old, during the 1998 All-Star Game.

16. True or False: The 1997–98 Milwaukee Bucks became the first team to score more than double their opponents' score, with a 124-59 win over the Trail Blazers.

17. Which team became the first former ABA team to win the NBA Finals in 1999?
    A. New Jersey Nets
    B. Indiana Pacers
    C. Denver Nuggets
    D. San Antonio Spurs

18. The Bulls missed the 1999 playoffs. How many years had it been since the last time they didn't make it in?
    A. 13
    B. 14
    C. 15
    D. 16

CHAPTER 11 ANSWERS:

1. B. Portland Trail Blazers. They led the Lakers by five games.
2. C. Japan. The Suns won 119-106 in the first game, then lost the second 102-101.
3. False. The Bulls defeated the Trail Blazers in 1992 to win the championship.
4. True. They missed the playoffs by seven games.
5. C. Charlotte Hornets. They defeated the Celtics to advance to the quarterfinals.
6. B. Phoenix Suns. The Bulls needed six games to win.
7. True. They selected Chris Webber in 1993, then traded him.
8. True. David Robinson scored 34 points, ten rebounds, ten assists, and ten blocks against the Pistons.
9. B. Houston Rockets. They won as the sixth seed in the Western Conference.
10. C. Orlando Magic. They were swept by the Rockets.
11. True. The Toronto Raptors and Vancouver Grizzlies joined the league in 1995.
12. True. He also won the MVP Triple Crown that year.
13. C. Five. He quickly established himself as a potent scorer.
14. B. Gregg Popovich. It was the start of the longest tenure in NBA coaching history.
15. True. Jordan won the MVP of the contest, though.
16. False. It was the Indiana Pacers that accomplished the feat.
17. D. San Antonio Spurs. They defeated the New York Knicks in the Finals.
18. C. 15. They were also the second defending champion to miss, as did the 1969–70 Celtics.

Did You Know?

A lockout shortened the 1998–99 season to 50 games.

CHAPTER 12:
THE 2000S

1. True or False: Doc Rivers became the first to win Coach of the Year without his team making the playoffs.

2. True or False: The Vancouver Grizzlies became the first Canadian team to make the playoffs in 2000.

3. The 2000–01 Lakers went on an incredible playoff run. How many playoff games did they lose?
   A. One
   B. Two
   C. Three
   D. Four

4. How many Western Conference teams won 40 or more regular season games but still missed the 2001 playoffs?
   A. One
   B. Two
   C. Three
   D. Four

5. True or False: Allen Iverson was the first scoring leader not to make the All-NBA First Team in 2002.

6. True or False: The 2001–02 season was the first to make the zone defense illegal.

7. Which player took MVP honors during the longest All-Star Game in league history, back in 2003?
   A. Allen Iverson
   B. Kevin Garnett
   C. Michael Jordan
   D. Tim Duncan

8. For the first time in league history, two ABA teams met in the Finals. Who did the Spurs beat for the title?
   A. Indiana Pacers
   B. Charlotte Hornets

C. Seattle SuperSonics
D. New Jersey Nets

9. True or False: Three teams with playoff appearance streaks of more than 20 years failed to make the playoffs in 2004.

10. True or False: LeBron James became the first rookie to lead a playoff team in scoring since David Robinson in 1990.

11. Mike D'Antoni won Coach of the Year in 2005 when he coached which team to the league's best record?

    A. Phoenix Suns
    B. Seattle SuperSonics
    C. Dallas Mavericks
    D. Miami Heat

12. Which rookie in 2004–05 became the only player to come straight from high school and start all 82 games in his rookie year?

    A. Emeka Okafor
    B. Dwight Howard
    C. Chris Paul
    D. Kevin Durant

13. True or False: In January 2006, Kobe Bryant scored 81 points against the Raptors, the second-most in a single game.

14. True or False: Both teams participating in the 2006 NBA Finals played in arenas sponsored by Delta Airlines.

15. The 2007 NBA All-Star Game was the first held in a non-NBA city. Where was it held?

    A. Buffalo
    B. Las Vegas
    C. St. Louis
    D. Kansas City

16. Which team became the first eight-seed to defeat the one-seed, beating the Mavericks in 2007?

    A. Golden State Warriors
    B. Los Angeles Lakers
    C. Denver Nuggets
    D. Houston Rockets

17. True or False: The Minnesota Timberwolves received seven players in exchange for Kevin Garnett, the biggest trade for one player in league history.

18. True or False: Phil Jackson passed Red Auerbach in 2009 with his tenth NBA championship victory as a coach.

CHAPTER 12 ANSWERS:

1. True. His Orlando Magic finished the 1999-2000 season with a 41-41 record.
2. False. The Toronto Raptors were the first Canadian team to make the playoffs, which they accomplished in 2000.
3. A. One. Their winning percentage would be bested by the 2017 Golden State Warriors.
4. C. Three. The SuperSonics, Nuggets, and Rockets all missed the playoffs despite their records.
5. True. He did make the Second Team, though.
6. False. 2001-02 was the first year the zone defense was legal.
7. B. Kevin Garnett. The game needed two overtimes to decide a winner.
8. D. New Jersey Nets. The Spurs won in six games.
9. False. Two teams with playoff streaks over 20 years missed the playoffs: Portland and Utah.
10. False. Carmelo Anthony led Denver's scoring in the 2004 playoffs.
11. A. Phoenix Suns. Having Steve Nash at point guard was a tremendous help.
12. B. Dwight Howard. He played every game for the Orlando Magic in his rookie year.
13. True. His performance was second only to Wilt's 100.
14. False. Both arenas were sponsored by American Airlines: Miami and Dallas.
15. B. Las Vegas. Kobe Bryant won the MVP award for the game.
16. A. Golden State Warriors. They beat Dallas in six games.
17. True. Garnett played 12 years in Minnesota before being traded to Boston.
18. True. The Lakers defeated the Magic in five games.

Did You Know?

Jose Calderon of the Raptors broke the league record for free throw percentage over a season when he finished the 2008-09 season with a 98.1%. He only missed three of 154 attempts!

CHAPTER 13:
THE 2010S

1. Ben Gordon of the Detroit Pistons helped the NBA reach which regular season milestone on January 9, 2010?

    A. One millionth point
    B. Five millionth point
    C. Ten millionth point
    D. 12 millionth point

2. On March 19, 2010, LeBron James became the youngest player to reach which milestone?

    A. 10,000 points
    B. 15,000 points
    C. 20,000 points
    D. 25,000 points

3. True or False: Phil Jackson announced his retirement after suffering the only playoff sweep of his career against the Mavericks in 2011.

4. True or False: Derrick Rose was awarded the 2011 league MVP award, as well as All-NBA First Team honors.

5. The 2011-12 NBA season started on what date because of a lockout?

    A. December 9
    B. December 14
    C. December 16
    D. December 25

6. Kevin Durant became the seventh player in history, and the latest since Michael Jordan in 1998, to do what in 2012?

    A. Three straight scoring titles
    B. Three straight Finals MVPs
    C. Three straight league MVPs
    D. Three straight All-Star MVPs

7. True or False: LeBron James eclipsed 20,000 points and 5,000 assists in the same game.

8. True or False: Gregg Popovitch became the first coach to 800 wins on March 22, 2013.

9. The San Antonio Spurs won the 2014 NBA Finals over the Miami Heat in how many games?
   A. Four
   B. Five
   C. Six
   D. Seven

10. Kevin Durant added his fourth scoring title in 2014, averaging how many points per game?
    A. 31
    B. 32
    C. 33
    D. 34

11. True or False: LeBron James returned to Cleveland in 2014 after five seasons with Miami.

12. True or False: The Knicks and Magic set an NBA record for fewest combined points in a quarter, with 15 during the second quarter of a game on April 11, 2015.

13. In 2015–16, the Golden State Warriors broke the NBA record with how many regular-season wins?
    A. 72
    B. 73
    C. 74
    D. 75

14. While the Warriors were breaking records in 2015–16, which team won 39 straight home games, second only to the Warriors' 54?
    A. Houston Rockets
    B. Cleveland Cavaliers
    C. San Antonio Spurs
    D. Oklahoma City Thunder

15. True or False: Klay Thompson was the first player to score 60 points in less than 30 minutes during the shot-clock era.

16. True or False: James Harden recorded the first 50-15-15 game in NBA history on December 31, 2016.

17. Which rookie became the only player to score 170 points, 100 rebounds, and 80 assists in his first ten games?
    A. Jayson Tatum
    B. Kyle Kuzma
    C. Donovan Mitchell
    D. Ben Simmons

18. Golden State swept which team to win the 2018 NBA Finals?
    A. Boston Celtics
    B. Cleveland Cavaliers
    C. Toronto Raptors
    D. Philadelphia 76ers

CHAPTER 13 ANSWERS:

1. C. Ten millionth point. It did not help the Pistons much with their season.
2. B. 15,000 points. James would also be the youngest to 25,000 points later in his career.
3. True. He had managed to find more success against every other playoff opponent.
4. True. He had a successful season with the Bulls.
5. D. December 25. Five games were played on Christmas Day to start the season.
6. A. Three straight scoring titles. He averaged 28 points per game in 2011–12.
7. True. He accomplished the feat on January 16, 2013.
8. False. He was the second coach to the milestone, after Jerry Sloan.
9. B. Five. Kawhi Leonard and Tony Parker helped foil LeBron James and the Heat.
10. B. 32. He skipped 2013 but won four scoring titles in five years.
11. False. James only played four years in Miami.
12. True. The two teams struggled to gain points and set the record in the history books.
13. B. 73. The previous record was 72, set by the 1995–96 Bulls.
14. C. San Antonio Spurs. Their streak was snapped by the Warriors.
15. True. He scored 60 in 29 minutes against the Pacers on December 5, 2016.
16. True. He accomplished the feat against the Knicks on December 31, 2016.
17. D. Ben Simmons. He would go on to win Rookie of the Year in 2018.
18. B. Cleveland Cavaliers. It was an intense rivalry for a few years.

Did You Know?

Giannis Antetokounmpo was named league MVP in 2019, but his team fell in the Eastern Conference Finals.

CHAPTER 14: DREAM TEAMS

1. True or False: Prior to the 1992 Olympics, the International Basketball Federation prevented professionals from playing for Olympic teams.

2. True or False: In the previous Olympic Games (1988), the U.S. finished third after a loss to Brazil.

3. Team USA decided to include one college player on their 1992 roster. Who was it?

   A. Shaquille O'Neal
   B. Christian Laettner
   C. Patrick Ewing
   D. Charles Barkley

4. Which player from the 1992 roster also competed on the 1988 iteration of the team?

   A. David Robinson
   B. Larry Bird
   C. Scottie Pippen
   D. John Stockton

5. True or False: Clyde Drexler was selected over Isiah Thomas for the final 1992 roster spot.

6. True or False: Michael Jordan was selected to be the public face of the 1992 Olympic team.

7. The Dream Team's first international competition was a 136-57 victory over which team at the Tournament of the Americas?

   A. Puerto Rico
   B. Venezuela
   C. Brazil
   D. Cuba

8. With a 127-80 victory against which team, Team USA won the Tournament of the Americas and qualified for the 1992 Olympics?

   A. Puerto Rico
   B. Venezuela

C. Brazil
D. Argentina

9. True or False: Dream Team Coach Chuck Daly said he didn't impose a curfew because he didn't want to adhere to it; he enjoyed walking along the beach at night.

10. True or False: The Dream Team didn't stay with the other Olympians, and instead stayed at a nearby hotel, taking up 80 of the 98 rooms.

11. An incident during the Dream Team's first game against Angola, involving which player, made fans view the American team as bullies instead of a very skilled team?

    A. Patrick Ewing
    B. Michael Jordan
    C. Charles Barkley
    D. Larry Bird

12. Besides Croatia, which was the only team to lose by less than 40 to the Dream Team?

    A. Puerto Rico
    B. Germany
    C. Lithuania
    D. Brazil

13. True or False: After a disappointing finish in the 2004 Olympics, the 2008 U.S. Men's Basketball team was dubbed "Dream Team Part Two."

14. True or False: LeBron James was named the captain of the 2008 Olympic team as they prepared to travel to China.

15. Which USA player was the team's leading scorer during the 2008 Olympics?

    A. Kobe Bryant
    B. Carmelo Anthony
    C. Chris Paul
    D. Dwyane Wade

16. While not as dominant as the 1992 team, who did the USA defeat with the largest winning margin during group play?

    A. Angola
    B. Germany

C. Spain
D. Greece

17. True or False: The Redeem Team won the gold medal game by only one point over Spain.

18. True or False: The Redeem Team roster featured 11 All-Stars.

CHAPTER 14 ANSWERS:

1. True. When the rule changed, it gave the U.S. a chance to dominate the game.
2. False. They lost to the Soviet Union and settled for bronze.
3. B. Christian Laettner. He was selected over O'Neal, who was also a college player at the time.
4. A. David Robinson. He was motivated to win a gold after falling short before.
5. True. Some thought it was because of bad blood between Thomas and Jordan, but nothing was ever confirmed.
6. False. Jordan declined the idea, so Larry Bird and Magic Johnson were named co-captains.
7. D. Cuba. After the game, Cuba's coach said, "You can't cover the sun with your finger."
8. B. Venezuela. The blowout wins made the Americans big favorites for gold.
9. False. He didn't impose a curfew because his favorite nightclub didn't open until midnight.
10. True. Fans and opponents both would gather outside in hopes of autographs and pictures.
11. C. Charles Barkley. He elbowed an opponent and was whistled for an intentional foul.
12. A. Puerto Rico. They lost 115-77.
13. False. The team was dubbed the "Redeem Team."
14. False. Kobe Bryant was named the captain of the team.
15. D. Dwyane Wade. He averaged 16 points per game.
16. B. Germany. They defeated Germany 106-57.
17. False. They defeated Spain by 11 points.
18. True. The NBA players did not hold back when asked to participate.

Did You Know?

Chris Bosh led the Redeem Team with 6.9 rebounds per game over the span of the tournament.

CHAPTER 15:
TEAMS ON THE MOVE

1. Starting with the BAA in 1946, which team was the first to move away from their initial location?

   A. Fort Wayne Pistons
   B. Rochester Royals
   C. Tri-Cities Blackhawks
   D. Minneapolis Lakers

2. Which NBA team was the first to find their permanent home through a move?

   A. Detroit Pistons
   B. Los Angeles Lakers
   C. Philadelphia 76ers
   D. Atlanta Hawks

3. True or False: The Syracuse Nationals moved to Philadelphia and became the 76ers in 1963.

4. True or False: When the Baltimore Bullets moved to Washington in 1973, they became known as the Washington Bullets.

5. These teams all moved in the late 1970s. Which of them moved last?

   A. Kansas City-Omaha Kings
   B. New York Nets
   C. Buffalo Braves
   D. New Orleans Jazz

6. The San Diego Clippers played for six seasons. How many playoff appearances did they make?

   A. Zero
   B. One
   C. Two
   D. Three

7. True or False: The Minneapolis Lakers made the playoffs 11 times in their 12 years in the league.

8. True or False: In the six seasons the Grizzlies played in Vancouver, their win percentage was a lowly .320.

9. At the time of their move, which team had the best win percentage of any team that had to move?

   A. Minneapolis Lakers
   B. Syracuse Nationals
   C. St. Louis Hawks
   D. Rochester Royals

10. Of all the teams that have moved over the years, which is the only team that made the playoffs every year before they moved?

    A. St. Louis Hawks
    B. Philadelphia Warriors
    C. Fort Wayne Pistons
    D. Syracuse Nationals

11. True or False: The Buffalo Braves moved in 1978 to New Orleans, creating the New Orleans Jazz.

12. True or False: The New York Nets played for eight seasons before moving to New Jersey.

13. Which team moved to New Orleans in 2002, but the city they left would get a new team two years later?

    A. Charlotte Hornets
    B. Seattle SuperSonics
    C. New Jersey Nets
    D. Kansas City Kings

14. The Kansas City Kings made four playoff appearances in how many seasons of play?

    A. Nine
    B. Ten
    C. 11
    D. 12

15. True or False: The New Orleans Hornets had to move to Kansas City temporarily because of Hurricane Katrina in 2005.

16. True or False: The Seattle SuperSonics moved to Oklahoma City after 31 seasons in the league.

17. The SuperSonics won how many titles before moving to Oklahoma City?

    A. One
    B. Two
    C. Three
    D. Four

18. How many seasons did the New Orleans Hornets last before changing their name to the Pelicans?

    A. Four
    B. Five
    C. Six
    D. Seven

CHAPTER 15 ANSWERS:

1. C. Tri-Cities Blackhawks. In 1951, they became the Milwaukee Hawks.
2. A. Detroit Pistons. They moved from Fort Wayne to Detroit in 1957, three years before the Lakers.
3. True. The team had made the playoffs every year, and won one championship, before the move.
4. False. In their first year in Washington, they were named the Capital Bullets.
5. New Orleans Jazz. They moved to Utah in 1979.
6. A. Zero. The team's overall winning percentage was only .378.
7. True. Fans still didn't show up to the games.
8. False. It was worse than that, at .220.
9. D. Rochester Royals. They had a .576 win percentage over nine seasons.
10. D. Syracuse Nationals. They made the playoffs in each of their 14 seasons.
11. False. The Braves moved to San Diego, creating the San Diego Clippers.
12. True. They only made one playoff appearance in that time.
13. A. Charlotte Hornets. The Charlotte Bobcats would swoop in two years after the Hornets leave.
14. B. Ten. It was not a terrible record, but they could not get attendance up.
15. False. They had to play most of their games in Oklahoma City.
16. False. They had been in the league for 41 years.
17. A. One. The team's win percentage was .524.
18. C. Six. The team's win percentage was .480 while named the Hornets.

Did You Know?

The Toronto Raptors had to play their home games in Tampa, Florida during the 2020 season because of the COVID-19 pandemic.

CHAPTER 16: DIVISIONAL CHANGES

1. True or False: The 1946–47 BAA season only featured two divisions, East and West.

2. True or False: The NBA had three divisions in the 1948–49 season.

3. The NBA's East division added one team from the NBL in 1949. Which one?

   A. Tri-Cities Blackhawks
   B. Indianapolis Olympians
   C. Fort Wayne Pistons
   D. Syracuse Nationals

4. After the BAA/NBL merger, five teams from the BAA's West division moved to the Central. Which of these did not move?

   A. Minneapolis Lakers
   B. Rochester Royals
   C. Anderson Packers
   D. St. Louis Bombers

5. True or False: After the 1970 expansion, there were four equal divisions in the league.

6. True or False: With the 1974 expansion, the Atlantic division added another team.

7. After the ABA merger, which of the four divisions added two teams, more than any other?

   A. Atlantic
   B. Central
   C. Midwest
   D. Pacific

8. One division didn't add any teams in the 1976 ABA merger. Which one?

   A. Atlantic
   B. Central
   C. Midwest

D. Pacific

9. True or False: The Pistons moved to the Central division after the Buffalo Braves moved to the Pacific division as the Clippers.

10. True or False: When the Jazz moved from New Orleans to Utah, the Bucks moved from the Midwest division to the Central.

11. Which team was placed in the Midwest division during the 1980 expansion?

    A. Denver Nuggets
    B. Houston Rockets
    C. Dallas Mavericks
    D. San Antonio Spurs

12. During the 1988 expansion, which division was left with one extra team?

    A. Atlantic
    B. Central
    C. Midwest
    D. Pacific

13. True or False: When the Kansas City Kings moved to Sacramento, they moved to the Pacific division.

14. True or False: The 1988 expansion added two teams to the league.

15. The 1989 expansion added two more teams, and after more shuffling, which division was left with one fewer team than the rest?

    A. Atlantic
    B. Central
    C. Midwest
    D. Pacific

16. Which team moved from the Atlantic division over to the Midwest division after the 1989 expansion?

    A. Minnesota Timberwolves
    B. San Antonio Spurs
    C. Charlotte Hornets
    D. Indiana Pacers

17. True or False: The Orlando Magic and Charlotte Hornets switched divisions in 1990.

18. True or False: The Magic spent two seasons in the Midwest division before moving to the Atlantic division.

CHAPTER 16 ANSWERS:

1. True. There were only 11 teams, and 6 were in the East.
2. False. The NBA only had two divisions in the 1948–49 season.
3. D. Syracuse Nationals. It would be the start of a great franchise.
4. C. Anderson Packers. They merged from the NBL, then left after one season.
5. False. There were four divisions, but they were not equal in size.
6. False. The new team went to the Central division.
7. C. Midwest. They added Denver and Indiana.
8. D. Pacific. They remained with five teams.
9. True. The Bullets also moved from the Central to the Atlantic.
10. False. The Pacers moved from the Midwest to the Central.
11. C. Dallas Mavericks. That left three divisions of equal size.
12. D. Pacific. The new teams were not added to that division, though.
13. False. They eventually made that move, but not for three years.
14. True. Charlotte and Miami were both added.
15. A. Atlantic. Every other division had seven teams.
16. C. Charlotte Hornets. The team would only be in that division for one season, though.
17. True. Orlando went to the Midwest, and Charlotte went to the Central.
18. False. The Magic only spent one season in the Midwest division.

Did You Know?

The NBA went from four divisions to six in 2004, even though only one new team was added to the league.

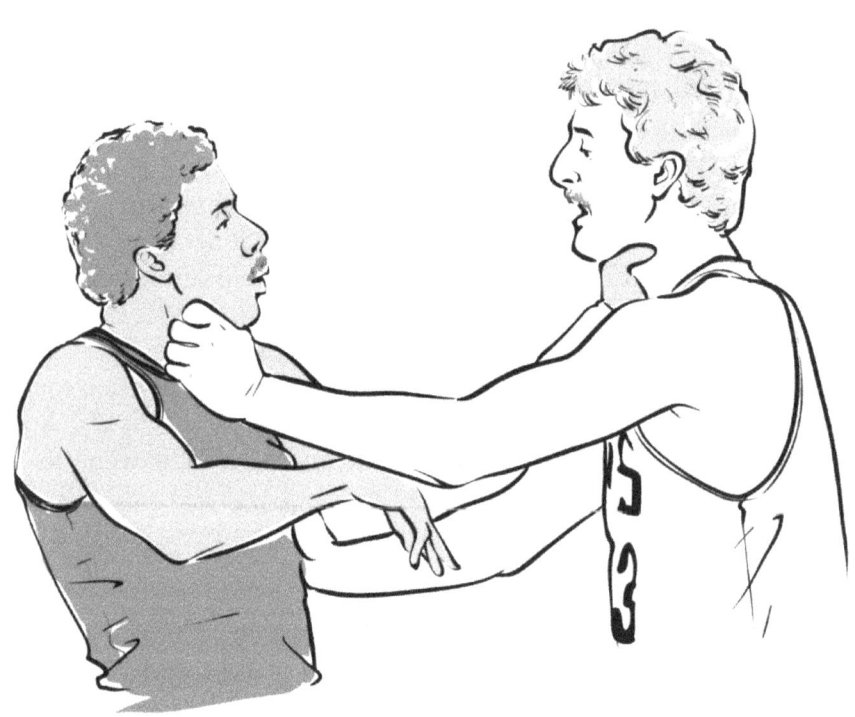

CHAPTER 17:
THE EASTERN CONFERENCE

1. True or False: The first time a trophy was awarded to the Eastern Conference champions was in 2001.

2. True or False: The Eastern Conference championship trophy was named after Bob Pettit.

3. In 2021-22, the Eastern Conference also began to award MVP honors for each of the Conference Finals matchups. Whose name is on the Eastern Conference Finals MVP trophy?

   A. Larry Bird
   B. John Havlicek
   C. Bill Russell
   D. Wilt Chamberlain

4. The Eastern Conference has produced how many NBA titles since 1970, its founding year?

   A. 23
   B. 24
   C. 25
   D. 26

5. True or False: The first Eastern Conference champion was the Baltimore Bullets.

6. True or False: The first NBA champion to rise from winning the Eastern Conference championship was the Boston Celtics in 1974.

7. What is the longest streak of NBA championships the Eastern Conference has won?

   A. Three
   B. Four
   C. Five
   D. Six

8. How many Eastern Conference champions have swept their NBA Finals opponents?

   A. One

B. Two
   C. Three
   D. Four

9. True or False: The Baltimore Bullets won the Eastern Conference championship with the worst record of any other Eastern Conference champion.

10. True or False: Only two Eastern Conference teams have failed to win an Eastern Conference championship, Atlanta, and Charlotte.

11. Three Eastern Conference teams have reached the NBA Finals four years in a row. Which of these teams has not accomplished that feat?

    A. Miami Heat
    B. Cleveland Cavaliers
    C. Chicago Bulls
    D. Boston Celtics

12. Three teams have won five Eastern Conference championships. Which of these teams hasn't accomplished that feat?

    A. Cleveland Cavaliers
    B. Detroit Pistons
    C. Philadelphia 76ers
    D. New York Knicks

13. True or False: The Boston Celtics have won the most Eastern Conference championships.

14. True or False: The Chicago Bulls have won more Eastern Conference championships than the Miami Heat.

15. Which Eastern Conference champion had the best record without winning the NBA Finals?

    A. 2008–09 Orlando Magic
    B. 1984–85 Boston Celtics
    C. 1974–75 Washington Bullets
    D. 1979–80 Philadelphia 76ers

16. After the conference's creation, which team was first to leave?

    A. Buffalo Braves
    B. Cincinnati Royals
    C. New Orleans Jazz

D. Houston Rockets

17. True or False: Six of the current Eastern Conference teams spent some amount of time in the Western Conference during their existence.

18. True or False: The first team to be presented with the Eastern Conference championship trophy was the Philadelphia 76ers.

CHAPTER 17 ANSWERS:

1. True. There was no trophy for reaching the NBA Finals before that season.
2. False. The trophy is named after Bob Cousy.
3. A. Larry Bird. The first winner was Jayson Tatum.
4. B. 24. Most recently, the Bucks won in 2021.
5. True. They were swept in the 1971 NBA Finals.
6. False. The New York Knicks won the title in 1973.
7. C. Five. The Pistons and Bulls won five titles between them from 1989 to 1993.
8. B. Two. The last team to do it was the Pistons in 1989.
9. True. Their regular season record was 42-40.
10. True. Meanwhile, the Pacers, Bucks, and Raptors have one each.
11. C. Chicago Bulls. They had two streaks of three with Michael Jordan.
12. D. New York Knicks. They've only won four.
13. True. They've won ten, most recently in 2022.
14. False. Miami has seven to Chicago's six.
15. B. 1984–85 Boston Celtics. They had 63 wins but couldn't finish the playoff run.
16. B. Cincinnati Royals. They left in 1972.
17. True. Chicago, Detroit, Indiana, Miami, Milwaukee, and Orlando.
18. True. They lost to the Los Angeles Lakers in the NBA Finals, though.

Did You Know?

The 1977–78 Washington Bullets won the NBA Finals with the worst record of any NBA champion from the Eastern Conference.

CHAPTER 18:
THE WESTERN CONFERENCE

1. Six organizations have been in the Western Conference since its inception in 1970. Which of these is not one of those organizations?

   A. Sacramento Kings
   B. Houston Rockets
   C. Portland Trail Blazers
   D. Phoenix Suns

2. True or False: The Memphis Grizzlies and Minnesota Timberwolves are the two eastern-most teams in the Western Conference.

3. True or False: The first team to ever leave the Western Conference was the Indiana Pacers.

4. Only one former ABA team is currently in the Western Conference. Which one is it?

   A. Los Angeles Clippers
   B. Denver Nuggets
   C. Oklahoma City Thunder
   D. Phoenix Suns

5. Which team was the only one to join the Western Conference as an expansion team in 1970, when the conference was formed?

   A. Golden State Warriors
   B. San Antonio Spurs
   C. Portland Trail Blazers
   D. Dallas Mavericks

6. True or False: The Milwaukee Bucks have more Western Conference championships than six Western Conference teams.

7. True or False: The Los Angeles Lakers have won more than double the Western Conference championships than the next closest team.

8. Which Western Conference champion holds the record for the best record?

   A. 1971–72 Lakers
   B. 2015–16 Warriors

C. 1999–00 Lakers
D. 1970–71 Bucks

9. Six organizations have been in the Western Conference since its inception in 1970. Which of these is not one of them?
   A. Sacramento Kings
   B. Houston Rockets
   C. Portland Trail Blazers
   D. Phoenix Suns

10. True or False: The Los Angeles Lakers were the first Western Conference champions to be swept in the NBA Finals.

11. True or False: The 1980–81 Houston Rockets are the only Western Conference champion to have a losing regular season record.

12. As of the summer of 2023, how many more NBA titles have Western Conference champions won over their Eastern Conference counterparts?
    A. Four
    B. Five
    C. Six
    D. Seven

13. Which Western Conference champion accomplished an NBA Finals sweep with the worst record?
    A. 1994–95 Rockets
    B. 1988–89 Lakers
    C. 2001–02 Lakers
    D. 2006–07 Spurs

14. True or False: The Phoenix Suns and Portland Trail Blazers have each won three Western Conference championships.

15. True or False: The Rockets only trail the Lakers and Warriors in Western Conference championships.

16. Which of these teams has not won two Western Conference titles, as of 2023?
    A. Utah Jazz
    B. Milwaukee Bucks
    C. Dallas Mavericks

D. Denver Nuggets

17. The Western Conference championship trophy is named after which NBA legend?

    A. Magic Johnson
    B. Wilt Chamberlain
    C. Oscar Robertson
    D. Clyde Drexler

18. True or False: The Western Conference Finals MVP award was named after Kareem Abdul-Jabbar.

CHAPTER 18 ANSWERS:

1. False. The Grizzlies and Hornets are the two eastern-most teams.
2. False. The Detroit Pistons left the Western Conference first, in 1978.
3. A. Sacramento Kings. They joined the conference in 1972 from the Eastern Conference.
4. B. Denver Nuggets. They joined the NBA in 1976.
5. C. Portland Trail Blazers. Every other team transferred from the old divisions or expanded later.
6. True. They won it twice, more than the Nuggets, Grizzlies, Timberwolves, Pelicans, Clippers, and Kings.
7. True. They've won 19 conference titles, and the next closest team has seven.
8. B. 2015-16 Warriors. They hold the NBA record with 73 wins to nine losses.
9. A. Sacramento Kings. They joined in 1972.
10. True. They lost the 1983 Finals to the Philadelphia 76ers.
11. True. The Rockets had a 40-42 record.
12. B. Five. The count is 29 to 24.
13. A. 1994-95 Rockets. They only won 47 regular season games on their way to the title.
14. True. The Suns reached the Finals most recently, in 2021.
15. False. They also trail the Spurs.
16. D. Denver Nuggets. They only have one.
17. C. Oscar Robertson. It was named after him during the 2021-22 season.
18. False. It was named after Magic Johnson in 2021-22.

Did You Know?
Both Florida teams spent time in the Western Conference.

CHAPTER 19:
ATLANTIC DIVISION

1. When the Atlantic Division formed in 1970, how many teams belonged to it?
   A. Four
   B. Five
   C. Six
   D. Seven

2. Which team has the most division titles in its history?
   A. New York Knicks
   B. Boston Celtics
   C. Philadelphia 76ers
   D. Brooklyn Nets

3. True or False: The only Atlantic Division team to win the NBA championship without winning the division was the 1972–73 Knicks.

4. True or False: Robert Parish has played more games for the Celtics than any other player.

5. While John Havlicek leads the Celtics in all-time points scored, which player is second?
   A. Larry Bird
   B. Robert Parish
   C. Kevin McHale
   D. Paul Pierce

6. Which Celtic has pulled down more rebounds for the team than anyone else?
   A. Robert Parish
   B. Dave Cowens
   C. Bill Russell
   D. Larry Bird

7. True or False: Brook Lopez leads the Nets in all-time points, just ahead of Buck Williams.

8. True or False: Jason Kidd has the most steals of any Nets player, with 950.

9. Which Nets player has played more games for the organization than any other player?

    A. Brook Lopez
    B. Buck Williams
    C. Mike Gminski
    D. Jason Collins

10. Which Knicks player leads the Knicks in points, rebounds, and games played?

    A. Walt Frazier
    B. Willis Reed
    C. Allan Houston
    D. Patrick Ewing

11. True or False: Walt Frazier leads the Knicks in all-time assists.

12. True or False: Bob McAdoo played three seasons with the Knicks and has the highest points per game average of any Knicks player.

13. Which 76er leads the organization in points all-time, with 15 seasons played?

    A. Allen Iverson
    B. Dolph Schaves
    C. Julius Erving
    D. Hal Greer

14. Which 76ers player from the 1950s and 60s leads the organization in total rebounds all-time?

    A. Red Kerr
    B. Dolph Schayes
    C. Charles Barkley
    D. Billy Cunningham

15. True or False: Two Philadelphia players, Julius Erving, and Samuel Dalembert, have more than 1,000 career blocks with the team.

16. True or False: DeMar DeRozan leads all Toronto Raptors in games played, with 675.

17. Which big man has more rebounds than any other Raptor in team history?

    A. Chris Bosh
    B. Jonas Valanciunas
    C. Pascal Siakam
    D. Kyle Lowry

18. Which player only spent one season in Toronto, but he holds the franchise record for points per game average?

    A. Vince Carter
    B. Kawhi Leonard
    C. RJ Barrett
    D. Mike James

CHAPTER 19 ANSWERS:

1. A. Four. Celtics, Braves, Knicks, and 76ers.
2. B. Boston Celtics. They have won 25.
3. True. Every other champion won the division on their way to the title.
4. False. Parish is second to John Havlicek.
5. D. Paul Pierce. He played 168 fewer games and scored 2,374 fewer points.
6. C. Bill Russell. He gathered over 10,000 more rebounds than the next closest player.
7. True. Lopez only has four more points than Williams.
8. True. Darwin Cook is in second, with 875.
9. B. Buck Williams. He played 635 games for the team, the only player with more than 600 games.
10. D. Patrick Ewing. He has 9,000 more points than Walt Frazier.
11. True. He accumulated 4,791 in ten seasons.
12. True. He averaged 26.7 points per game.
13. D. Hal Greer. He is the only 76er with more than 20,000 points for the team.
14. B. Dolph Schayes. He's the only 76er with more than 10,000 rebounds.
15. True. Caldwell Jones has 926, too.
16. True. Kyle Lowry is second with 601.
17. A. Chris Bosh. He had 4,776 rebounds with the team.
18. B. Kawhi Leonard. He averaged 26.6 points per game.

Did You Know?

The Atlantic Division champions receive the Nat "Sweetwater" Clifton Trophy.

CHAPTER 20: CENTRAL DIVISION

1. True or False: The Central Division has had 13 NBA champions.

2. True or False: In the 2005–06 season, every team from the Central Division made the playoffs.

3. Which player holds the Bulls' record for points per game average?
   A. DeMar DeRozan
   B. Zach LaVine
   C. Jalen Rose
   D. Michael Jordan

4. Which Bulls player leads the organization in blocks all-time?
   A. Artis Gilmore
   B. Michael Jordan
   C. Joakim Noah
   D. Scottie Pippen

5. True or False: Kirk Hinrich leads the Bulls in all-time three-pointers, as of 2023.

6. True or False: LeBron James leads the Cavaliers in points all-time, by more than 12,000.

7. Which Cavalier has the most blocks for the organization?
   A. Hot Rod Williams
   B. Larry Nance
   C. Zydrunas Ilgauskas
   D. LeBron James

8. LeBron James does not lead the Cavaliers in which of these categories?
   A. Offensive rebounds
   B. Assists
   C. Steals
   D. Turnovers

9. True or False: Isiah Thomas has played more games than any other Pistons player.

10. True or False: Andre Drummond leads the Pistons in all-time rebounds.

11. Which Detroit Piston leads the organization in blocks?

    A. Terry Tyler
    B. Andre Drummond
    C. Ben Wallace
    D. Bob Lanier

12. Reggie Miller leads in many categories, but not which one?

    A. Assists
    B. Total rebounds
    C. Steals
    D. Turnovers

13. True or False: Myles Turner leads the Pacers in all-time blocks.

14. True or False: Reggie Miller's three-point shooting percentage was .433.

15. Which player leads all Milwaukee Bucks in games played for the organization?

    A. Junior Bridgeman
    B. Khris Middleton
    C. Giannis Antetokounmpo
    D. Sidney Moncrief

16. Which Bucks player leads the team in all-time steals?

    A. Quinn Buckner
    B. Giannis Antetokounmpo
    C. Paul Pressey
    D. Sidney Moncrief

17. Giannis leads the Bucks in rebounds, but which player is second?

    A. Bob Dandridge
    B. Kareem Abdul-Jabbar
    C. Marques Johnson
    D. Andrew Bogut

18. True or False: The Central Division champion is awarded the Wayne Embry Trophy.

CHAPTER 20 ANSWERS:

1. True. The Bulls won six of those.
2. True. None of those teams would win the NBA Finals, though.
3. D. Michael Jordan. He averaged 31.5 points per game.
4. A. Artis Gilmore. His 4,277 assists are 507 more than Calderon.
5. True. Zach LaVine is within 60 of catching him, as of 2023–24.
6. True. He scored 23,119 in 11 seasons.
7. C. Zydrunas Ilgauskas. He has 1,269 blocks in 12 years.
8. A. Offensive rebounds. Ilgauskas has more than LeBron.
9. False. Joe Dumars has more games with the Pistons.
10. False. Bill Laimbeer has more rebounds, 9,430.
11. C. Ben Wallace. He grabbed 1,486 blocks in nine seasons.
12. B. Total rebounds. That category belongs to Mel Daniels, with 7,643 in only six seasons.
13. True. He passed Jermaine O'Neal.
14. False. His three-point shooting percentage was only .395. Still impressive.
15. C. Giannis Antetokounmpo. Bridgeman played 711 games, but Giannis passed him.
16. A. Quinn Buckner. He leads with 1,042 steals as of 2023.
17. B. Kareem Abdul-Jabbar. Giannis has over 7,600 to Kareem's 7,161.
18. True. Embry played for the Royals, Bucks, and Celtics.

Did You Know?

The "Central Division" existed previously, for one season, back in 1949–50.

CHAPTER 21: SOUTHEAST DIVISION

1. True or False: The Southeast Division was created in 2004 when the New Orleans Hornets joined the league.

2. True or False: The Earl Lloyd Trophy is awarded to the Southeast Division champion.

3. Between them, the two Florida teams won the division how many years in a row?

   A. 9
   B. 10
   C. 11
   D. 12

4. Which Hawks player leads the organization in games played, though his last year with the team was in 1994?

   A. Dominique Wilkins
   B. Tree Rollins
   C. Bob Pettit
   D. Kevin Willis

5. True or False: Mookie Blaylock leads the Hawks in all-time assists.

6. True or False: Bob Pettit leads the Hawks organization in total rebounds.

7. Which Hornets player leads the organization in games played?

   A. Muggsy Bogues
   B. Kemba Walker
   C. Dell Curry
   D. Cody Zeller

8. Which Hornets player leads the organization in points, only playing eight seasons there?

   A. Gerald Wallace
   B. Kemba Walker
   C. Dell Curry
   D. Larry Johnson

9. True or False: Muggsy Bogues leads the Hornets in all-time steals.

10. True or False: Udonis Haslem has played the most games for the Miami Heat.

11. Which player has more than double the blocks of the player who is second on the list?
    A. Alonzo Mourning
    B. Dwyane Wade
    C. Hassan Whiteside
    D. Rony Seikaly

12. Which Heat player, who is on the 2023–24 roster, leads the organization in all-time three-pointers made?
    A. Tim Hardaway
    B. Eddie Jones
    C. Tyler Herro
    D. Duncan Robinson

13. True or False: Nick Anderson has played more games for the Orlando Magic than anyone else.

14. True or False: Nikola Vucevic leads the Magic in all-time points scored.

15. Which Magic player leads the organization in all-time assists?
    A. Scott Skiles
    B. Darrell Armstrong
    C. Jameer Nelson
    D. Anfernee Hardaway

16. Which player leads the Wizards organization in games played, though his last season was in 1981?
    A. Wes Unseld
    B. Elvin Hayes
    C. Bradley Beal
    D. Greg Ballard

17. True or False: Bradley Beal leads the Wizards in all-time points.

18. True or False: John Wall leads the Wizards in all-time steals.

CHAPTER 21 ANSWERS:

1. False. The division was created when the Charlotte Bobcats joined the league.
2. True. Lloyd helped the Syracuse Nationals win the 1955 NBA title.
3. B. Ten. Atlanta broke the streak in 2015.
4. A. Dominique Wilkins. He played 882 games in 12 seasons.
5. False. Doc Rivers leads at the time of this book's publication, but Trae Young is close behind.
6. True. He collected 12,849 rebounds in 11 seasons.
7. C. Dell Curry. He played 701 games with the organization.
8. B. Kemba Walker. He has 12,009 points in eight years.
9. True. He collected 1,067 in ten seasons with the team.
10. False. Dwyane Wade has played 948 games to Haslem's 879.
11. A. Alonzo Mourning. He had 1,625 blocks in 11 seasons.
12. D. Duncan Robinson. He passed Hardaway, who had 806 in six years.
13. True. He played 692 games over ten seasons.
14. False. Dwight Howard leads the organization with 11,435 points.
15. C. Jameer Nelson. He collected 3,501 assists in ten seasons.
16. A. Wes Unseld. He played 984 games in 13 seasons.
17. False. Elvin Hayes leads Beal by less than 200 points.
18. True. He had 976 steals in nine seasons.

Did You Know?

The Heat have won the division 12 out of 19 times, as of 2023.

CHAPTER 22:
NORTHWEST DIVISION

1. The SuperSonics/Thunder and which team are tied with six division titles each, as of 2023?

    A. Trail Blazers
    B. Timberwolves
    C. Nuggets
    D. Jazz

2. The Northwest Division trophy is named after which Hall of Fame player?

    A. Bill Russell
    B. K.C. Jones
    C. John Havlicek
    D. Sam Jones

3. True or False: The Northwest Division is geographically the most expansive in the league.

4. True or False: Alex English leads all Denver Nuggets in games played with the organization.

5. This Nugget leads which organization in blocks, with 1,486?

    A. Bobby Jones
    B. Wayne Cooper
    C. Dikembe Mutombo
    D. Marcus Camby

6. Which Nugget leads the organization in assists and rebounds?

    A. Alex English
    B. Nikola Jokic
    C. Fat Lever
    D. Andre Miller

7. True or False: Kevin Garnett has played more games in a Timberwolves jersey than anyone else.

8. True or False: Karl-Anthony Towns leads the Timberwolves organization in all-time three-pointers made.

9. In his four years with the Timberwolves, Terrell Brandon averaged 8.3 what per game, tied for the highest in team history?

   A. Steals
   B. Rebounds
   C. Assists
   D. Free throws made

10. Which Thunder/SuperSonic player got to 999 games with the organization, the team record?

    A. Fred Brown
    B. Nick Collison
    C. Russell Westbrook
    D. Gary Payton

11. True or False: Russell Westbrook leads the team with 18,859 points scored.

12. True or False: Serge Ibaka collected 1,100 blocks to lead the team.

13. Which Trail Blazer still leads the team in games played all-time?

    A. Jerome Kersey
    B. Clyde Drexler
    C. Damian Lillard
    D. Terry Porter

14. Which player leads the Trail Blazers in most points all-time?

    A. Jerome Kersey
    B. Clyde Drexler
    C. Damian Lillard
    D. Terry Porter

15. True or False: Terry Porter has more assists than any other Trail Blazer.

16. True or False: John Stockton has played more games for the Jazz than anyone else.

17. Though Stockton played one more season, which player leads the Jazz in all-time points?

    A. Adrian Dantley
    B. Darrell Griffith
    C. Karl Malone

D. Thurl Bailey

18. Which Jazz player has more blocks than any other?
    A. Andrei Kirilenko
    B. Rudy Gobert
    C. Greg Ostertag
    D. Mark Eaton

CHAPTER 22 ANSWERS:

1. C. Nuggets. Denver's victory in 2023 brought them to six.
2. D. Sam Jones. He was part of the Celtics greatness of the 1960s.
3. True. It covers more land than any other division.
4. True. He played 837 games in 11 seasons, from 1980 to 1990.
5. C. Dikembe Mutombo. He played five seasons with the team.
6. B. Nikola Jokic. He has played nine seasons with the team and counting.
7. True. He played 970 games in 14 seasons.
8. True. He's made more than 970 so far, and Anthony Edwards is about 200 behind him.
9. C. Assists. He's tied with Stephon Marbury for the top spot.
10. D. Gary Payton. He played 13 seasons with the team.
11. True. He has about 650 more than Gary Payton.
12. False. Ibaka leads the organization with 1,300 blocks in seven seasons.
13. B. Clyde Drexler. He played 867 games in 12 seasons.
14. C. Damian Lillard. He scored 19,376 points in 11 seasons.
15. True. He collected 5,319 assists in ten seasons.
16. True. He played 1,504 games in 19 years with the team.
17. C. Karl Malone. He scored 36,374 points in 18 seasons.
18. D. Mark Eaton. He amassed 3,064 blocks in 11 seasons.

Did You Know?

Besides the SuperSonics moving to Oklahoma City, the teams in the Northwest Division have remained unchanged since its inception in 2003–04.

CHAPTER 23: PACIFIC DIVISION

1. True or False: The Lakers have won 28 division titles.
2. True or False: The Clippers have only won two division titles.
3. How many of the five Pacific Division teams made the playoffs in 2023?
   A. Two
   B. Three
   C. Four
   D. Five
4. Which Warrior has played the most games for the organization?
   A. Stephen Curry
   B. Chris Mullin
   C. Draymond Green
   D. Klay Thompson
5. True or False: Wilt Chamberlain leads the Warriors organization in all-time rebounds.
6. True or False: Only one Warrior has ever collected more than 1,000 blocks for the team.
7. Which Clippers player leads the organization in games played?
   A. Randy Smith
   B. DeAndre Jordan
   C. Eric Piatkowski
   D. Loy Vaught
8. Which Clippers guard has more assists in six years than any other player in team history?
   A. Randy Smith
   B. Gary Grant
   C. Chris Paul
   D. Norm Nixon
9. True or False: Paul George has made more three-pointers than any other Clipper.

10. True or False: Kareem Abdul-Jabbar leads the Lakers in all-time games played.

11. Which is the only Lakers player to collect more than 10,000 assists?
    A. Kobe Bryant
    B. Jerry West
    C. Norm Nixon
    D. Magic Johnson

12. Which Laker collected more rebounds than any other?
    A. Elgin Baylor
    B. Kareem Abdul-Jabbar
    C. Kobe Bryant
    D. Magic Johnson

13. True or False: Walter Davis has played more games for the Suns than any other player.

14. True or False: Before the 2023–24 season, Walter Davis led the Suns in all-time points.

15. Which Suns player has 940 blocks, the most all-time for the team?
    A. Mark West
    B. Larry Nance
    C. Shawn Marion
    D. Alvan Adams

16. Which Kings player leads the organization in games played?
    A. Jack Twyman
    B. Oscar Robertson
    C. Sam Lacey
    D. Adrian Smith

17. True or False: Oscar Robertson leads the Kings organization with 7,731 career assists.

18. True or False: Buddy Hield leads the Kings in three-pointers made.

CHAPTER 23 ANSWERS:

1. False. They have won 24.
2. True. They won in 2013 and 2014.
3. D. Five. The Kings won the division with 48 wins that year.
4. A. Stephen Curry. He's played over 900 games and counting, into 2024.
5. False. Nate Thurmond leads the team with 12,771 rebounds in 11 seasons.
6. True. Adonal Foyle earned 1,140 blocks in ten seasons.
7. B. DeAndre Jordan. He played 750 games in ten seasons.
8. C. Chris Paul. He had 4,023 assists in those six seasons.
9. True. He made 792 in five seasons.
10. False. Kobe Bryant has played the most Lakers games, with 1,346.
11. D. Magic Johnson. He had 10,141 assists in 13 years.
12. A. Elgin Baylor. He had 11,463 rebounds in 14 years.
13. False. Alvan Adams leads all Suns in games played, with 988 in 13 years.
14. True. Though, Devin Booker is likely to surpass him soon.
15. B. Larry Nance. He played seven seasons for the team.
16. C. Sam Lacey. He played 888 games in 12 seasons.
17. True. Lacey is next on the list, at 3,563.
18. True. He made 1,248 in six seasons.

Did You Know?
The Pacific Division trophy is named after Hall of Famer Chuck Cooper.

CHAPTER 24:
SOUTHWEST DIVISION

1. True or False: The Spurs won the NBA Finals in their first season as part of the Southwest Division.

2. True or False: The Spurs are the only team from the Southwest Division to win the NBA Finals.

3. Which team has the fewest Southwest Division titles?

    A. New Orleans Hornets/Pelicans
    B. Memphis Grizzlies
    C. Dallas Mavericks
    D. Houston Rockets

4. True or False: Dirk Nowitzki has played more games as a Maverick than anyone else.

5. Which Maverick leads the organization in career assists, with 5,111?

    A. Brad Davis
    B. Jason Kidd
    C. Derek Harper
    D. Luka Doncic

6. Nowitzki leads the Mavericks in most blocks all-time, but which player is a close second?

    A. Shawn Bradley
    B. James Donaldson
    C. Erick Dampier
    D. Kurt Nimphius

7. True or False: Calvin Murphy has played more games than any other Rocket.

8. True or False: James Harden leads the Rockets in three-pointers all-time.

9. Which Rocket leads the organization in points scored all-time?

    A. James Harden
    B. Calvin Murphy
    C. Rudy Tomjanovich

D. Hakeem Olajuwon

10. Which Grizzlies player has played more games than anyone else, as of 2023?

    A. Mike Conley
    B. Marc Gasol
    C. Zach Randolph
    D. Rudy Gay

11. True or False: Marc Gasol leads the Grizzlies in rebounds all-time.

12. True or False: Through 2024, Ja Morant leads the Grizzlies with 22.5 points per game, the highest all-time.

13. Which New Orleans Pelican/Hornet has played 530 games, the organization's most?

    A. Anthony Davis
    B. Chris Paul
    C. David West
    D. Jrue Holiday

14. Anthony Davis leads the Pelicans/Hornets in many categories, but which one doesn't he?

    A. Rebounds
    B. Points
    C. Assists
    D. Blocks

15. True or False: Chris Paul is the only Pelican with more than 700 steals.

16. True or False: Tony Parker leads the Spurs in all-time games played.

17. Which Spurs player leads the team in all-time steals?

    A. David Robinson
    B. Manu Ginobili
    C. George Gervin
    D. Alvin Robertson

18. Which Spurs player collected 6,829 assists while with the team?

    A. Tony Parker
    B. Avery Johnson
    C. Tim Duncan
    D. Manu Ginobili

CHAPTER 24 ANSWERS:

1. True. They won the division again in 2005-06 but lost in the second round.
2. True. They have done it twice since 2004-05.
3. A. New Orleans Hornets/Pelicans. They have won one, in 2008.
4. True. He played 1,522 games in 21 seasons.
5. C. Derek Harper. He played 12 seasons with the team.
6. A. Shawn Bradley. He had 31 fewer blocks in 12 fewer seasons.
7. False. Hakeem Olajuwon has played 1,177 games in 17 seasons, 175 more than Murphy.
8. True. He made 2,029 in nine seasons.
9. D. Hakeem Olajuwon. He scored 26,511 points in 17 seasons.
10. A. Mike Conley. He played 788 games, 19 more than Marc Gasol.
11. True. He had 5,942 rebounds in 11 seasons.
12. True. He's played five seasons with the team.
13. C. David West. He played eight seasons for the team.
14. C. Assists. He leads in every other category listed, only playing seven seasons with the team.
15. True. He has 1,010 steals in six seasons.
16. False. Tim Duncan played the most games, 1,392.
17. B. Manu Ginobili. He collected 1,392 steals in 16 seasons.
18. A. Tony Parker. He played 17 seasons to get those assists.

Did You Know?
The Southwest Division trophy is named after Hall of Famer Willis Reed.

CHAPTER 25:
THE NBA FINALS

1. True or False: The winner of the NBA Finals is awarded the Walter A. Brown Trophy.

2. True or False: From 1950 to 1985, the Finals were called the NBA World Championship Series.

3. As of 2023, how many NBA teams have won the NBA Finals at some point in their history?
   A. 20
   B. 21
   C. 22
   D. 23

4. The Lakers and Celtics are tied, both having won how many NBA Finals?
   A. 15
   B. 16
   C. 17
   D. 18

5. True or False: The NBA Finals used a 2-3-2 games format from 1985 to 2014.

6. True or False: The Lakers have reached the Finals more than any other team.

7. Which NBA team has the most Finals appearances without a championship?
   A. New Jersey/Brooklyn Nets
   B. Phoenix Suns
   C. Orlando Magic
   D. Utah Jazz

8. The Lakers have lost 15 NBA Finals. The 76ers and which team are tied for the second-most losses?
   A. Celtics
   B. Warriors

C. Pistons
   D. Knicks

9. True or False: The Spurs have a better win percentage in the NBA Finals than the Celtics.

10. True or False: The Baltimore Bullets are the only team that has won a championship and no longer exists.

11. Which is the only NBA team with multiple championships that has never lost in the NBA Finals?

    A. Chicago Bulls
    B. San Antonio Spurs
    C. Sacramento Kings
    D. Milwaukee Bucks

12. Which championship-winning team has the worst NBA Finals win percentage?

    A. Thunder/SuperSonics
    B. Wizards/Bullets
    C. Cavaliers
    D. Hawks

13. True or False: Clyde Drexler never won an NBA Finals with the Trail Blazers.

14. True or False: The SuperSonics are the only team since 1977 to win a title and then move.

15. Which NBA franchise has been around the longest with no Finals appearances?

    A. Los Angeles Clippers
    B. Minnesota Timberwolves
    C. Memphis Grizzlies
    D. Charlotte Hornets

16. Only one NBA team, as of 2023, has a winning percentage of .500 for NBA Finals games. Which team is it?

    A. Houston Rockets
    B. Dallas Mavericks
    C. Los Angeles Lakers
    D. Philadelphia 76ers

17. True or False: The Dallas Mavericks have only ever faced the Miami Heat in the NBA Finals.

18. True or False: Jerry West has more trips to the Finals than any other player.

CHAPTER 25 ANSWERS:

1. False. The current trophy is called the Larry O'Brien Championship Trophy.
2. True. As of 2023, it is called the NBA Finals presented by YouTube TV.
3. B. 21. The Nuggets won it most recently, in 2023.
4. C. 17. The Lakers won it in 2020; the Celtics in 2008.
5. True. The team with the better record played at home for Games 1, 2, 6, and 7.
6. True. They have reached the Finals 32 times.
7. B. Phoenix Suns. They are zero-for-three in the Finals.
8. D. Knicks. Both the Knicks and 76ers have lost six Finals.
9. True. The Spurs have a .833 win percentage in the Finals to the Celtics' .773.
10. True. Every other NBA championship team still exists, even if they moved.
11. A. Chicago Bulls. They won six in the 1990s, and they never lost in the Finals.
12. C. Cavaliers. Their win percentage is .200.
13. True. He lost twice with the team that drafted him.
14. True. They won in 1979 and then left in 2008.
15. A. Los Angeles Clippers. They have played 54 seasons with no trips to the Finals.
16. B. Dallas Mavericks. They are 6-6 in NBA Finals games.
17. True. The two meetings were in 2006 and 2011.
18. False. Bill Russell has the most trips to the Finals, with 12.

Did You Know?

As of 2023, the Lakers have played more NBA Finals games than any other team, and they are 93-92 in those games.

CHAPTER 26:
BASKETBALL HALL OF FAME

1. True or False: The Naismith Basketball Hall of Fame was established in 1958.

2. True or False: The first class of inductees was selected in 1968.

3. Which NBA team has the most inductees to the Hall?

   A. Los Angeles Lakers
   B. Boston Celtics
   C. New York Knicks
   D. Atlanta Hawks

4. For how many years was the Hall of Fame facility located at Springfield College?

   A. 15
   B. 16
   C. 17
   D. 18

5. True or False: The first women were inducted into the Hall in 1981.

6. True or False: Besides spots in the Hall of Fame, the Hall also presents awards to college basketball players.

7. Which trophy is presented to the top NCAA Division I Men's point guard?

   A. Jerry West Award
   B. Julius Erving Award
   C. Kareem Abdul-Jabbar Award
   D. Bob Cousy Award

8. Which trophy is presented to the top NCAA Division I Women's center?

   A. Nancy Lieberman Award
   B. Ann Meyers Drysdale Award
   C. Lisa Leslie Award
   D. Cheryl Miller Award

9. True or False: Only Henry V. Porter was inducted in 1960 as a contributor, after seven people were inducted in 1959.

10. True or False: Walter A. Brown was inducted in 1965, and he was well known for founding the New York Knicks.

11. Who was the shoe salesman inducted in 1969 for running the first basketball clinic at North Carolina State University?

   A. Charles H. Taylor
   B. Abraham M. Saperstein
   C. Robert L. Douglas
   D. William G. Mokray

12. Which of these players was inducted into the Hall of Fame first?

   A. Bill Russell
   B. Bob Cousy
   C. Elgin Baylor
   D. Wilt Chamberlain

13. True or False: Larry Bird was inducted into the Hall four years before Magic Johnson.

14. Who was the first Olympic gold medalist inducted into the Hall of Fame as a player?

   A. Bill Russell
   B. Tom Gola
   C. Jerry West
   D. Bob Kurland

15. True or False: The first international player inducted was Sergei Belov, in 1990.

16. Which woman, inducted in 1996, was the first to compete in a men's league?

   A. Joan Crawford
   B. Nancy Lieberman
   C. Denise Curry
   D. Lynette Woodward

17. True or False: John Wooden was the first to be inducted as both a player and a coach.

18. True or False: Only twice has the Hall inducted individuals without selecting a player.

CHAPTER 26 ANSWERS:

1. False. The Hall was established in 1959.
2. False. The first inductees were selected in 1959, but the Hall didn't physically open until 1968.
3. B. Boston Celtics. They have 40 inductees.
4. C. 17. It then moved to a new facility in 1985.
5. False. The first women were inducted in 1985.
6. True. There are five awards for both the men's and women's college players.
7. D. Bob Cousy Award. It has been presented to one player annually since 2004.
8. C. Lisa Leslie Award. It was first awarded in 2018.
9. True. Porter edited the first high school rule book from 1936.
10. False. He was the founder of the Boston Celtics.
11. A. Charles H. Taylor. The Chuck Taylor "All-Star" is one of the most popular shoes of the era.
12. B. Bob Cousy. He was inducted in 1971.
13. True. Larry was inducted in 1998; Magic in 2002.
14. D. Bob Kurland. He was inducted in 1961.
15. False. Belov was inducted in 1992.
16. B. Nancy Lieberman. She played for USBL Springfield in 1986.
17. True. Player: 1960, Coach: 1973.
18. False. There have been three such occasions: 1965, 1968, and 2007.

Did You Know?

The Frances Pomeroy Naismith Award is presented to the country's best college basketball player under a specific height. (Men – 6ft or shorter)

CHAPTER 27: SCORING CHAMPIONS

1. True or False: A player must play in 60 regular season games to be considered eligible for the scoring title.

2. True or False: The 1968-69 season was the last time the scoring champion was determined by total points and not by points per game.

3. Which scoring champion holds the NBA record for most points in a single season?
   A. Michael Jordan
   B. James Harden
   C. Wilt Chamberlain
   D. Allen Iverson

4. Who was the first scoring champion not to be inducted into the Hall of Fame?
   A. Joe Fulks
   B. Max Zaslofsky
   C. George Mikan
   D. Paul Arizin

5. True or False: The first player to average more than 30 points per game was Wilt Chamberlain in 1959-60.

6. True or False: George Mikan was the first to repeat as scoring champion, back in 1950.

7. Who was the first to win the scoring title and the league MVP?
   A. Bob Pettit
   B. Paul Arizin
   C. Wilt Chamberlain
   D. George Yardley

8. How many scoring titles did Wilt Chamberlain win in a row?
   A. Four
   B. Five
   C. Six
   D. Seven

9. True or False: Wilt Chamberlain is the only player to average over 50 points per game for a season.

10. True or False: Bob McAdoo was a member of the New Orleans Jazz when he won three scoring titles in a row.

11. Which Spurs player won three scoring titles from 1978 to 1980?

    A. Pete Maravich
    B. George Gervin
    C. Adrian Dantley
    D. Alex English

12. Both Paul Arizin and which player won scoring titles five years apart?

    A. Russell Westbrook
    B. James Harden
    C. Stephen Curry
    D. Kevin Durant

13. True or False: Michael Jordan won 11 scoring titles during his time in the league.

14. True or False: Kobe Bryant's 2006 scoring title season averaged more points than James Harden's 2019 scoring title season.

15. After Zaslofsky's 1948 title, who won the scoring title with the fewest free throws made?

    A. Stephen Curry in 2021
    B. Allen Iverson in 1999
    C. Tracy McGrady in 2004
    D. Alex English in 1983

16. Which player is the only one to make more than 400 three-pointers on their way to a scoring title?

    A. Stephen Curry
    B. James Harden
    C. Russell Westbrook
    D. Kevin Durant

17. True or False: Only Michael Jordan and Wilt Chamberlain have scored more than 3,000 points in a season to win the scoring title.

18. True or False: Kevin Durant was the youngest player to win a scoring title, at 22 years old.

CHAPTER 27 ANSWERS:

1. False. They must play in 58 regular season games, with some special rules that allow fewer.
2. True. This helped even out players who played in a different number of games.
3. C. Wilt Chamberlain. He scored 4,029 points in 1961–62.
4. B. Max Zaslofsky. Fulks would have won if they had used points per game and not total points.
5. True. He averaged 37.6 points that season.
6. True. He also won it a third time in a row, in 1951.
7. A. Bob Pettit. He won both in 1956.
8. D. Seven. He won them from 1960 to 1966.
9. True. He accomplished the feat in 1961–62.
10. False. He played for the Buffalo Braves.
11. B. George Gervin. He was also the first to win the title with three-pointers included.
12. C. Stephen Curry. He won it in 2016 and 2021.
13. False. He won it ten times.
14. False. Harden averaged 36.1 to Kobe's 35.4.
15. B. Allen Iverson in 1999. He only made 356 free throws.
16. A. Stephen Curry. In 2016, he made 402 three-pointers.
17. True. Wilt did it three times, Jordan once.
18. False. Durant was 21 when he won the scoring title for the first time.

Did You Know?

Russell Westbrook is the only player to win the scoring title while averaging a triple-double on the season.

CHAPTER 28:
THE SIXTH MAN AWARD

1. True or False: The Sixth Man Award was first presented in 1983.

2. True or False: To be eligible for the award, a player must come off the bench for one-third of a season's games.

3. Which player was awarded the first Sixth Man Award in 1983?

   A. Bobby Jones
   B. Kevin McHale
   C. Bill Walton
   D. Ricky Pierce

4. Which player was the first to repeat as the Sixth Man Award winner?

   A. Ricky Pierce
   B. Kevin McHale
   C. Detlef Schrempf
   D. Jamal Crawford

5. True or False: Ben Gordon was the first rookie to win the award in 2005.

6. True or False: Lou Williams is the only player to win the award four times.

7. Jamal Crawford played for how many years between his first and second Sixth Man Awards?

   A. Two
   B. Three
   C. Four
   D. Five

8. Who was the first non-American to win the Sixth Man Award?

   A. Leandro Barbosa
   B. Manu Ginobili
   C. Detlef Schrempf
   D. Toni Kukoc

9. True or False: Mike Miller is the only rookie to win the award.

10. True or False: Manu Ginobili is the only player to win the award and be named to an All-NBA Team in the same season.

11. Which team has had more Sixth Man winners than any other team?

    A. Boston Celtics
    B. New York Knicks
    C. Dallas Mavericks
    D. Los Angeles Clippers

12. Montrezl Harrell is one of two centers to win the Sixth Man Award. Who is the other?

    A. Ricky Pierce
    B. Bill Walton
    C. Roy Tarpley
    D. Eddie Johnson

13. True or False: As of 2023, Manu Ginobili is the most recent Sixth Man winner to be inducted into the Hall of Fame.

14. True or False: Jamal Crawford is the only player to win the Sixth Man with two different teams.

15. Which of these Sixth Man winners is not a Hall of Famer?

    A. Kevin McHale
    B. Bill Walton
    C. Toni Kukoc
    D. Jason Terry

16. Who was the first point guard to win the Sixth Man Award?

    A. Toni Kukoc
    B. Clifford Robinson
    C. Darrell Armstrong
    D. Rodney Rogers

17. True or False: Small forwards have won more Sixth Man Awards than any other position.

18. True or False: The most recent point guard to win the Sixth Man, as of 2023, is Bobby Jackson in 2003.

CHAPTER 28 ANSWERS:

1. True. It wouldn't receive a player-dedicated name for several years.
2. False. A player must come off the bench more often than he starts.
3. A. Bobby Jones. He played for the 76ers and would go on to make the Hall of Fame.
4. B. Kevin McHale. He won it in 1984 and 1985.
5. True. He was a shooting guard for the Bulls at the time.
6. False. Williams won it three times.
7. C. Four. He won it in 2010 and 2014.
8. C. Detlef Schrempf. He won the award in 1991.
9. False. Malcolm Brogdon also won it as a rookie.
10. True. He was named to the Third Team that season (2008).
11. D. Los Angeles Clippers. They have had five winners.
12. B. Bill Walton. He won it in 1986.
13. True. He was inducted in 2022.
14. True. He won with the Hawks and Clippers.
15. D. Jason Terry. The other three are all Hall of Famers.
16. C. Darrell Armstrong. He won with the Magic in 1999.
17. False. Shooting guards have won most of the Sixth Man Awards.
18. True. He played for the Kings that season.

Did You Know?
Only five players have won the Sixth Man Award more than once.

CHAPTER 29: BIGGEST NCAA TOURNAMENT MOMENTS

1. True or False: In the 2009 tournament, Villanova upset Pitt thanks to point guard Scotty Reynolds dribbling the length of the court and making a running shot with less than a second left.

2. True or False: NC State won the national championship in 1983 with a last-second putback from Dereck Whittenburg, beating Ohio State.

3. Christian Laettner made "The Shot" to help which team reach the Elite 8 in 1992?
   A. North Carolina
   B. Duke
   C. Kentucky
   D. Michigan State

4. Keith Smart helped which team win the 1987 National Championship with a baseline jumper?
   A. Indiana
   B. North Carolina
   C. Duke
   D. Clemson

5. True or False: Derrick Rose missed a crucial free throw in the 2008 championship game, allowing Mario Chalmers to tie the game with a three-pointer.

6. True or False: Tyus Edney helped Boise upset UCLA in the 1995 NCAA tournament with a coast-to-coast drive with less than five seconds on the clock.

7. Danny Ainge scored on a play called "The Drive" in the 1981 tourney. Which team did he defeat with the famous play?
   A. Notre Dame
   B. Georgia
   C. Florida
   D. Indiana

8. In the 2012 tournament, Norfolk State upset which team in the first round?

   A. Mississippi State
   B. Missouri
   C. Florida
   D. Gonzaga

9. True or False: VCU upset Duke in 2007, then beat Pitt in overtime to reach the Sweet 16.

10. True or False: In 2005, Illinois had a great run thanks to Deron Williams, losing in the National Championship Game to North Carolina.

11. In the 2005 tourney, Vermont upset which team in the first round?

    A. Syracuse
    B. Oklahoma
    C. Kentucky
    D. Duke

12. Which college team has the most NCAA tournament championships?

    A. Kentucky
    B. North Carolina
    C. UCLA
    D. UConn

13. True or False: Mike Krzyzewski has won the most NCAA championships as a coach.

14. True or False: UConn has never lost an NCAA Championship Game.

15. Which of these teams has not reached the NCAA Championship Game 12 times?

    A. North Carolina
    B. Duke
    C. UCLA
    D. Kentucky

16. Which of these teams has not lost six NCAA Championship Games?

    A. North Carolina
    B. Duke
    C. Kentucky

D. Kansas

17. True or False: As of 2023, Kansas holds the record for consecutive tournament appearances.

18. True or False: Shaquille O'Neal holds the NCAA record for most blocks in an NCAA tournament game.

CHAPTER 29 ANSWERS:

1. True. Villanova would lose to North Carolina in the next round.
2. False. NC State defeated Houston.
3. B. Duke. "The Shot" helped Duke defeat Kentucky.
4. A. Indiana. His winning shot came with three seconds left in the game.
5. True. Rose would find great success in the NBA, at least for a while.
6. False. Edney helped UCLA avoid an upset against Boise.
7. A. Notre Dame. His successful time at BYU was followed by a good career in the NBA.
8. B. Missouri. They lost to Florida in the second round, but it was still a surprising victory.
9. False. They upset Duke but lost to Pitt in overtime.
10. True. They defeated Louisville and Arizona on their way to the final game.
11. A. Syracuse. Vermont won the game 60-57.
12. C. UCLA. They have 11 championships, and no other team has 10.
13. False. John Wooden has ten titles, twice as many as Coach K.
14. True. UConn is 5-0 in Championship Games.
15. B. Duke. They have reached 11 title games.
16. C. Kentucky. They have lost four.
17. True. They've been to 33 straight tournaments.
18. True. He had 11 blocks in 1992 against BYU.

Did You Know?
UCLA reached the Final Four ten years in a row, from 1967 to 1976.

CHAPTER 30: UNBEATABLE RECORDS

1. True or False: Wilt Chamberlain is the only player in NBA history to score 100 points in a single game.

2. True or False: Klay Thompson holds the NBA record for most points in a single quarter, with 37.

3. Which of these percentages represents Jose Calderon's free throw shooting in 2008-09?

   A. 96.4
   B. 97.9
   C. 98.1
   D. 98.7

4. Which team averaged a record 126.5 points per game in the 1981–82 season?

   A. Indiana Pacers
   B. Boston Celtics
   C. Denver Nuggets
   D. Milwaukee Bucks

5. True or False: Michael Jordan and Wilt Chamberlain both ended their careers averaging 30.1 points per game, highest in league history.

6. True or False: Jordan won the scoring title ten years in a row, a record.

7. Which Boston Celtics player has played more games than any other player in history?

   A. Kareem Abdul-Jabbar
   B. Robert Parish
   C. Vince Carter
   D. Dirk Nowitzki

8. Which of these players has played in the most NBA seasons?

   A. Kareem Abdul-Jabbar
   B. Robert Parish
   C. Vince Carter
   D. Dirk Nowitzki

9. True or False: Wilt Chamberlain holds the record for average minutes played per game over a career.

10. True or False: Wilt Chamberlain is the only player to average 20 points and 20 rebounds per game in his career.

11. Who holds the ironman record, for most consecutive NBA games played?

    A. A.C. Green
    B. Randy Smith
    C. Johnny "Red" Kerr
    D. Michael Cage

12. Which NBA player has the most career steals? And it's not a close contest!

    A. Jason Kidd
    B. John Stockton
    C. Chris Paul
    D. Michael Jordan

13. True or False: John Stockton is the career leader in assists with 15,806.

14. True or False: Dikembe Mutombo is the career leader in blocks, with 3,289.

    Who is the only player to have scored more than 40,000 career points?

15. A. Kareem Abdul-Jabbar
    B. Karl Malone
    C. Kobe Bryant
    D. LeBron James

16. Which player holds the distinction as the league's shortest player ever?

    A. Earl Boykins
    B. Spud Webb
    C. Muggsy Bogues
    D. Chauncey Billups

17. True or False: Bill Russell has the most championships as a player, with 11.

18. True or False: Elmore Smith holds the single-game record with 14 blocks.

CHAPTER 30 ANSWERS:

1. True. His Philadelphia Warriors defeated the New York Knicks 169-147.
2. True. The record was once held by George Gervin of the Spurs.
3. C. 98.1 He made 151 of 154 during that season.
4. C. Denver Nuggets. They finished fourth in the conference despite the high-flying offense.
5. True. Luka Doncic sits in third as of 2024.
6. True. Joel Embiid has won two in a row as of 2023.
7. B. Robert Parish. He played 1,611 games in 21 seasons.
8. C. Vince Carter. He is the only player with 22 seasons of NBA play, though LeBron James is one season away, as of 2024.
9. True. His average of 45.8 minutes per game is 3.5 minutes ahead of Bill Russell, in second place.
10. True. No other player comes close to his numbers.
11. A. A.C. Green. He played 1,192 games in a row. The closest current player is Mikal Bridges at 454 games.
12. B. John Stockton. He has 3,265 steals. Chris Paul is the closest active player, but he is more than 600 behind.
13. True. The next closest player is more than 3,000 behind.
14. False. Hakeem Olajuwon is the career leader in blocks with 3,830. The closest active player is Brook Lopez, with 1,891.
15. D. LeBron James. As of 2024, he's not done yet.
16. C. Muggsy Bogues. He was five feet, three inches during his time in the league.
17. True. Even LeBron James only has four.
18. False. He recorded 17 blocks. Two players have tallied 15, but none have come closer.

Did You Know?

Dale Ellis holds the NBA record for minutes played with 69 minutes in a single game, back in the 1989 season.

CHAPTER 31:
THE BIGGEST MOMENTS

1. True or False: In the 1960 NBA Finals, the Celtics needed double overtime to win Game 7 over the Hawks and continue their streak of championships.

2. True or False: Elgin Baylor scored an NBA Finals record 61 points against the Celtics in Game 5 of the 1962 NBA Finals.

3. Who is the only NBA player to be named Finals MVP despite being on the losing side?
   A. Bill Russell
   B. Kareem Abdul-Jabbar
   C. Jerry West
   D. Willis Reed

4. Which Knick played through a torn tensor muscle to inspire his teammates to a Game 7 victory in the 1970 NBA Finals?
   A. Willis Reed
   B. John Havlicek
   C. Darryl Dawkins
   D. Kareem Abdul-Jabbar

5. True or False: Magic Johnson played in Kareem Abdul-Jabbar's position during the 1980 Finals, helping the Lakers win Game 6.

6. True or False: Larry Bird notched a triple-double, with 47 points, all with his non-dominant left hand.

7. Which Houston Rocket made a circus-like jumper to beat the Lakers and reach the 1986 NBA Finals?
   A. Hakeem Olajuwon
   B. Ralph Sampson
   C. Rodney McCray
   D. Craig Ehlo

8. Which player scored a record 25 points in the third quarter of Game 6 during the 1988 Finals on a bad ankle?
   A. Isiah Thomas

B. Magic Johnson
   C. Joe Dumars
   D. Kareem Abdul-Jabbar

9. True or False: Dubbed "The Shot," Michael Jordan's foul-line jumper in the 1989 playoffs eliminated the New York Knicks.

10. True or False: The Cavaliers refused handshakes after the Bulls defeated them in the 1991 playoffs.

11. Which player won the 1992 All-Star MVP despite retiring from the NBA months earlier?

    A. Hakeem Olajuwon
    B. Magic Johnson
    C. Julius Erving
    D. Kareem Abdul-Jabbar

12. Which SuperSonic unleashed a revenge dunk - considered one of the most savage dunks in playoff history - in the 1992 playoffs, sending Alton Lister to the floor?

    A. Eddie Johnson
    B. Shawn Kemp
    C. Benoit Benjamin
    D. Tony Brown

13. True or False: Reggie Miller scored eight points in nine seconds to defeat the Knicks in 1995.

14. True or False: The Knicks and Heat met in the playoffs every year from 1997 to 2000, which included brawls in 1997 and 1998.

15. "The Flu Game" was which game of the 1997 NBA Finals, when Michael Jordan scored 38 points while sick?

    A. Three
    B. Four
    C. Five
    D. Six

16. Which Piston chased down Reggie Miller to block a breakaway layup in the 2004 playoffs, helping the Pistons reach the NBA Finals?

    A. Ben Wallace
    B. Richard Hamilton

C. Chauncey Billups
D. Tayshaun Prince

17. True or False: Kobe Bryant scored 81 points in a January 2006 game, the closest anyone has come to 100 since Wilt.

18. True or False: LeBron James scored his team's final 15 points to beat the Pistons in Game 5 of the 2007 East Finals.

CHAPTER 31 ANSWERS:

1. True. It was an epic moment in league history.
2. True. Baylor and the Lakers won the game but lost the series in seven games.
3. C. Jerry West. He was the 1969 Finals MVP, though his Lakers fell to the Celtics.
4. A. Willis Reed. He only scored four points in Game 7, but his presence was enough to help.
5. True. Many saw it as a changing of the guard in Los Angeles.
6. True. He scored 47 points in the game during the 1985–86 season.
7. B. Ralph Sampson. The Rockets would lose to the Celtics in the Finals, but it denied the Lakers a fifth straight Finals.
8. A. Isiah Thomas. The Lakers would end up winning in seven games.
9. False. "The Shot" eliminated the Cavaliers.
10. False. The Pistons walked off the court in 1991, skipping handshakes after losing to the Bulls.
11. B. Magic Johnson. He retired after he received an HIV diagnosis.
12. B. Shawn Kemp. The dunk made up for the fight sparked earlier in the series.
13. True. The furious comeback helped his team overcome the Knicks and advance in seven games.
14. True. It was one of the best rivalries in the NBA.
15. C. Five. Jordan's illness gained national attention as he powered through to victory.
16. D. Tayshaun Prince. It was an early version of a play LeBron James would make years later.
17. True. He scored 55 in the second half.
18. False. He scored his team's final 25 points.

Did You Know?

Ray Allen hit a miracle three-pointer to save the Heat in the 2013 NBA Finals. The Spurs nearly defeated the Big Three until Allen came to the rescue.

CHAPTER 32: THE ALL-STAR GAME

1. True or False: The first All-Star Game was in March 1951.

2. True or False: Wilt Chamberlain scored 38 points in the 1962 All-Star Game, a record that lasted for over 50 years.

3. Which Cincinnati Royal was a reserve for the 1966 All-Star Game but earned MVP honors?

   A. Oscar Robertson
   B. Adrian Smith
   C. John Havlicek
   D. Rick Barry

4. The 1972 All-Star Game ended with a buzzer-beater from which legendary player?

   A. Bill Russell
   B. Oscar Robertson
   C. Wilt Chamberlain
   D. Jerry West

5. True or False: Julius Erving was named MVP in the first All-Star Game after the merger with the ABA.

6. True or False: Marvin Gaye performed a now-famous rendition of "The Star-Spangled Banner" at the 1983 All-Star Game, one year before he passed away.

7. Who is the only NBA coach ever ejected from an All-Star Game?

   A. Red Holzman
   B. Jack Ramsay
   C. Red Auerbach
   D. Don Nelson

8. In the 1984 All-Star Game, which player was the leading scorer but not the MVP?

   A. Isiah Thomas
   B. Julius Erving
   C. Magic Johnson

D. Larry Bird

9. True or False: Michael Jordan won the 1988 Slam Dunk Contest, then scored 40 points in the All-Star Game.

10. True or False: The 1997 All-Star Game honored the Top 25 players of all time with a ceremony.

11. Which All-Star was the first to score a triple-double in an All-Star Game?

    A. Allen Iverson
    B. Jason Kidd
    C. Michael Jordan
    D. Kobe Bryant

12. Which player sparked a fourth-quarter comeback in the 2001 All-Star Game, earning him MVP honors?

    A. Tim Duncan
    B. Allen Iverson
    C. Kobe Bryant
    D. Stephon Marbury

13. True or False: Despite their rivalry, Shaq and Kobe shared MVP honors at the 2009 All-Star Game.

14. True or False: At the 2011 All-Star Game, LeBron James tallied a triple-double and captured the MVP honors.

15. At the 2014 All-Star Game, which player impressed LeBron James, then united with him in Cleveland?

    A. Kyrie Irving
    B. Kevin Love
    C. Serge Ibaka
    D. Pau Gasol

16. Which player broke Wilt's record in 2017, scoring 52 points and earning MVP honors?

    A. LeBron James
    B. Steph Curry
    C. Kevin Durant
    D. Anthony Davis

17. True or False: The 2020 All-Star Game took place just three weeks after the passing of Kobe Bryant and his daughter, Gianna.

18. True or False: Steph Curry set the All-Star Game record in 2022 with six three-pointers in one quarter.

CHAPTER 32 ANSWERS:

1. True. It was held at the Boston Garden and had over 10,000 fans in attendance.
2. False. He scored 42 points but did not win Game MVP.
3. B. Adrian Smith. He led all scorers with 24 points.
4. D. Jerry West. He also won the MVP for his performance.
5. True. However, his team did not win that night.
6. True. The performance was used in a Nike commercial for the 2008 Olympic Games.
7. C. Red Auerbach. He also holds NBA records for ejections as a coach.
8. B. Julius Erving. He was closer to retiring than the other players but still put on a show.
9. True. It was a dominant weekend for the superstar.
10. False. The 1997 All-Star Game honored the Top 50 players for the league's 50th anniversary.
11. C. Michael Jordan. He accomplished the feat in 1997.
12. B. Allen Iverson. He scored 15 of his 25 points in the fourth quarter.
13. True. Kobe scored 27, and Shaq went eight-for-nine from the floor.
14. False. LeBron did have a triple-double, but Kobe Bryant won his fourth MVP.
15. A. Kyrie Irving. He went 14-of-17 from the field that night.
16. D. Anthony Davis. The West beat the East 192-182.
17. True. The teams wore Kobe's 24 and Gianna's two to honor them during the game.
18. True. He also set the record for most threes in a half, and in a game, with eight and 16.

Did You Know?

Only Kobe Bryant and Bob Pettit have amassed four All-Star MVP awards in their careers.

CHAPTER 33:
SCANDALS AND MODERN HEADLINES

1. True or False: A controversial dress code went into effect during the 2007 season.

2. True or False: The Grizzlies were sold in 2001, and the new owner changed his mind on keeping the team in Vancouver.

3. Which player controversially choked his head coach and threatened to kill him in 1997?

   A. Erick Dampier
   B. Muggsy Bogues
   C. Latrell Sprewell
   D. Adonal Foyle

4. A brawl took place between the Detroit Pistons, their fans, and which team in November 2004?

   A. New York Knicks
   B. Indiana Pacers
   C. Milwaukee Bucks
   D. Chicago Bulls

5. True or False: The Knicks and Nuggets fought in December of 2006, resulting in seven players being suspended.

6. True or False: The NBA added an age limit to the rules in 2005, stating that players entering the league must be two years out of high school before entering the draft.

7. What did the NBA crack down on in 2006–07, resulting in an initial spike of technical fouls and ejections?

   A. Intentional fouls
   B. Flagrant fouls
   C. Player complaints
   D. Jumping fouls

8. Larry Bird claimed that 'which' game of the 1984 NBA Finals was refereed unfairly in favor of the Lakers?

A. Game 3
B. Game 4
C. Game 5
D. Game 6

9. True or False: In Game 6 of the 1988 NBA Finals, Isiah Thomas was whistled for a phantom foul on Kareem Abdul-Jabbar, costing the Pistons the game.

10. True or False: Mike Bibby didn't get a call when Kobe Bryant bloodied his nose with an elbow in Game 6 of the 2002 Western Conference Finals.

11. Which coach was fined $100,000 in 2005 for his accusations of cheating against his player, Yao Ming?

    A. Mike Montgomery
    B. Rick Carlisle
    C. Mike D'Antoni
    D. Jeff Van Gundy

12. After Game 5 of the 2006 NBA Finals, Mavericks owner Mark Cuban was fined what amount for screaming at Commissioner David Stern that "[his] league is rigged"?

    A. $100,000
    B. $250,000
    C. $500,000
    D. $750,000

13. True or False: Tim Duncan was assessed a technical foul by referee Joey Crawford for laughing while sitting on the bench in a 2006-07 game.

14. True or False: A microfiber ball was used for part of the 2006-07 season, causing more turnovers and better shooting percentages.

15. Which referee was caught gambling on games he refereed, leading to 15 months in prison?

    A. Tim Donaghy
    B. Joey Crawford
    C. Scott Foster
    D. Tony Brothers

16. With the Denver Nuggets winning the 2023 NBA Finals, which player captured the Finals MVP?

    A. Michael Porter Jr.
    B. Nikola Jokic
    C. Bam Adebayo
    D. Jimmy Butler

17. True or False: Joel Embiid captured the 2023 scoring title and the league MVP.

18. True or False: The Orlando Magic selected Victor Wembanyama first overall in the 2023 NBA Draft.

CHAPTER 33 ANSWERS:

1. False. The dress code went into effect in 2005, only loosening around 2020.
2. True. A bidding war between four cities ended with Memphis getting the team.
3. C. Latrell Sprewell. He was suspended for 68 games for his conduct.
4. B. Indiana Pacers. The NBA suspended nine players for a combined 146 games.
5. True. They were suspended for a combined 47 games.
6. False. The age limit stated that players needed to be one year out of high school and be 19 years old.
7. C. Player complaints. Carmelo Anthony was infamously ejected on opening night that season.
8. D. Game 6. The Lakers won Game 6, but Bird and the Celtics still won Game 7.
9. False. Bill Laimbeer was whistled for the controversial foul.
10. True. The Kings lost Games 6 and 7 to the Lakers.
11. D. Jeff Van Gundy. His Rockets lost to the Mavericks in seven games.
12. B. $250,000. His team lost to the Heat in six games.
13. True. Crawford was suspended and assigned to anger management courses.
14. True. Players complained until the league reverted to leather balls.
15. A. Tim Donaghy. He would later release a book with his side of the story.
16. B. Nikola Jokic. Jokic scored 28 in the decisive Game 5.
17. True. His 76ers did not win in the playoffs, though.
18. False. Wembanyama was selected by the San Antonio Spurs with the first pick.

Did You Know?

The Golden State Warriors won the 2022 NBA Finals, with Stephen Curry claiming another Finals MVP in the process.

CHAPTER 34:
BASKETBALL STATISTICS AND ACRONYMS

1. GS. It is not Golden State, but it represents how important you are to your team.
2. MP. Not the Military Police, but a measurement of time, instead.
3. FGA. A high number in this stat could mean you are really good or really bad.
4. eFG%. It is a fancy stat that helps balance out different shooters.
5. ORB. Just give me another chance!
6. STL. It is not the city of St. Louis. It has more to do with thievery.
7. TOV. The "T" does not stand for time, though yours will go down if you have a lot of these.
8. PF. It does not mean "Points For."
9. VORP. Can your team play better with you on the bench?
10. OWS. How many games does your shooting affect?
11. TS%. There are lots of ways to score, and they're all important.
12. PER. It has nothing to do with points per game.
13. 3PAr. Okay, but how often are you trying to do that?
14. USG%. It is not related to the United States.
15. Dist. It is not a passing stat.
16. WS/48. It is not a crime TV show, but another efficiency stat.
17. OBPM. It is not related to heartbeats.
18. TRB. It does not mean "treble," though the ground may shake when some of these occur.

CHAPTER 34 ANSWERS:

1. Games Started. If you're a starter, you're pretty important to the team, right?
2. Minutes Played. Big-time players play big-time minutes.
3. Field Goals Attempted. A player can shoot a lot, but if they're not scoring, it doesn't help.
4. Effective Field Goal Percentage. After all, three-pointers are worth more than two-pointers.
5. Offensive Rebounds. When your team doesn't score the first time, another possession is huge.
6. Steals. Unexpected turnovers can give your team a big advantage.
7. Turnovers. If you don't take care of the ball, you generally don't win.
8. Personal Fouls. If you take too many, it will cost your team dearly.
9. Value Over Replacement Player. How much are you contributing to wins on the court?
10. Offensive Win Share. It tells you how many games you helped your team win with offense.
11. True Shooting Percentage. It measures shooting from the field and from the foul line.
12. Player Efficiency Rating. It measures per-minute production.
13. Three-Point Attempt Rate. It tells how many of your shots come from behind the arc.
14. Usage Percentage. It shows how many team plays utilized a player while they were playing.
15. Average Distance of Field Goal Attempt. How close are they to the basket?
16. Win Shares Per 48 Minutes. It shows how many wins a player adds to their team's record for every 48 minutes they play.
17. Offensive Box Plus/Minus. It shows how many points a player scores per 100 possessions compared to an average.
18. Total Rebounds. Offensive and defensive boards combined, showing a player's dominance at the rim.

Did You Know?

Steals were not recorded in the NBA until 1973.

CONCLUSION

Well, there you have it! Thirty-four chapters of pure basketball knowledge at your fingertips. This book covered some of the biggest names and most noteworthy accomplishments throughout the history of the sport. We started with the game's creator and how it grew over time, and we also looked closely at some of the teams and leagues that did not quite make it to today's game.

With the modern game, we examined some of the strongest performances by individual players and teams that proved their strength could carry on for years. With players like Larry Bird, Magic Johnson, Kareem, Michael, and Hakeem, there was plenty of material to work with! That's not even mentioning the biggest names of the most recent few years, like Kobe Bryant, LeBron James, Stephen Curry, and Nikola Jokic.

Knowing how the game has changed over the decades, and how the leagues of the past influenced how the game was played, are important cornerstones when it comes to understanding and respecting how the sport functions in today's world. The players are stronger, faster, and smarter than they were 100 years ago, and there are many more talented players able to join the ranks of the best league in the world.

When the game changes, it can enshrine older records in place for generations. It is unlikely, for example, that anyone will score 100 points in a game ever again. Moments like those are worth remembering because today's game does not provide those opportunities.

If you struggled with some of these chapters, be sure to revisit them and test yourself again. After all, your friends will never know that you memorized some of the most obscure and detailed moments of their favorite game. Then, when you unleash everything you have learned, you're sure to gain some respect off the court.

Thank you for reading this book. Pass it along to a friend when you've conquered every chapter and continue spreading the love of the game of basketball!